Sergei Prokofiev

Titles in the series Critical Lives present the work of leading cultural figures of the modern period. Each book explores the life of the artist, writer, philosopher or architect in question and relates it to their major works.

In the same series

Sergei Prokofiev

Christina Guillaumier

REAKTION BOOKS

For Josephine, André, Sophia and Philippa

Published by Reaktion Books Ltd
Unit 32, Waterside
44–48, Wharf Road
London N1 7UX, UK
www.reaktionbooks.co.uk

First published 2024
Copyright © Christina Guillaumier 2024

Printed and bound in Great Britain by Bell & Bain, Glasgow

A catalogue record for this book is available from the British Library

ISBN 978 1 78914 951 7

Contents

Note on Transliteration

The system of transliteration used throughout is American Library Association – Library of Congress, a system accepted among Slavists, as well as literary scholars and historians. For reference, the transliteration of the Russian alphabet is set out below. The main exceptions to this usage are accepted spellings of names and places, for example, Prokofiev, Rachmaninov and Koussevitzky.

а	a	с	s
б	b	т	t
в	v	у	u
г	g	ф	f
д	d	х	kh
е/ё	e	ц	ts
ж	zh	ч	ch
з	z	ш	sh
и/й	i	щ	shch
к	k	ъ	"
л	l	ы	y
м	m	ь	'
н	n	э	e
о	o	ю	iu
п	p	я	ia
р	r		

Introduction: Prokofiev and Russia

We, free Scythian nomads, blissfully roving,
Cherishing only liberty, holding it dear.
We build no temples, revere no gods, moving
From East to West, like the dark rays of prayers.
Konstantin Balmont, 'Scythians'[1]

One of the persistent conceptions of Sergei Prokofiev is that he was
the artist who erred; the prodigal son; the one who left Russia and
returned when the West had spurned him and refused to recognize
his gifts. The truth, in as far as we can now ascertain, was far more
sophisticated and complicated. This biography aims to bring a
cohesive approach to the constituent parts of his splintered life and
to shed some light on events behind the scenes. Questions continue
to be asked about his reasons for returning to the Soviet Union
at what, to an outsider's eyes, seemed an inauspicious time. We
wonder what compelled him to leave a seemingly comfortable life
in the West for the insecurities of an artistic life in the burgeoning
Soviet Union. But perhaps we are asking the wrong question; we
should be considering what specific artistic challenges he faced
as a composer–pianist working in the paradigm-shifting musical
world of the early to mid-twentieth century. Behind the facade and
the long-established narratives, how much do we know about the
composer's musical aspirations and artistic motivations? What
do we know about his obsession and collaboration with other art
forms, such as theatre and literature, which he constantly drew
upon for inspiration? How much of his aesthetics and artistry were

influenced by his essential self-identification as a Russian composer, whose primary source of inspiration came from the literature of his homeland, which he knew as Imperial Russia and would later revisit and re-experience as Soviet Russia.

As well as Prokofiev's published diaries, correspondence and sketches, other primary resources are now available to us in archives across the world. These allow us to illuminate some of the more complex decisions and reasoning that governed the composer's seemingly unexpected or even irrational decisions, such as returning to the Soviet Union when he did. The original sources also give us a sense of his aesthetics and artistic compass. As we shall see, Prokofiev was nothing if not rational; he made every decision with care and consideration like the chess player he was. He placed a premium on his own gifts, creativity, processes and practices. To suggest otherwise, or to undertake an analysis of his life without bearing this firmly in mind, would be to do him a terrible injustice.

As we shall see through previously unpublished letters to friends and colleagues, throughout his life, Prokofiev self-identified as Russian.[2] In the formulation best encapsulated by Elena Dubinets:

> émigré composers approach the topic of expatriation and national self-identification from a variety of positions. The perspectives differ according to their place of residence, their ethnicity (whether ethnic Russians or not), national identification (whether still Russian citizens or not), and their fundamental relationship to Russia (whether they consider themselves Russian composers or not).[3]

This is evident in his lived experiences, in his aesthetic choices and the company he kept, rather than through some textbook understanding of nationhood, which was anathema to him. He saw himself as a cosmopolitan, a Russian without borders. His approach to self-defining and operating as a Russian is evident and variously nuanced throughout his life in almost all the decisions he made, both for himself and for his family.[4] He understood himself as

Russian through his strong cultural roots, which he was immersed in intensely during his early education in Imperialist Petersburg. He had a deep love and understanding of the Russian language and its linguistic components, collaborating with poets of the day such as Konstantin Balmont and Valery Bryusov, to create a text-setting that he was satisfied with. He even wrote short stories in Russian. In the months following graduation from the St Petersburg Conservatory he travelled across Imperial Russia, concertizing, catching up with friends and looking for opportunities to make music and have others perform his music. His copious correspondence demonstrates how he kept in contact with as many of his Russian friends as he could, asking for and receiving the latest scores and books being written on music.[5]

These connections were extremely valuable to him. In many ways, they were Prokofiev's umbilical cord to his version of Russia, the Imperial Russia that he knew and loved in his youth and early adulthood. He was influenced by Russian thought and critical ideas throughout his career. At no point did he consciously create a break in his aesthetic thinking from his Russian forebears or from his musical preferences and traditions. Russia's rich musical legacy remained his compositional compass, even if he reconfigured and defamiliarized ideas in his own inimitable style. The imprint of his musical heritage is unmistakable and runs through his entire oeuvre, regardless of the period he was writing in. This Russian flavour or musical essence can be heard in his musical turns of phrase, his robust use of octatonicism and his colourful textures, connecting his music directly to Nikolai Rimsky-Korsakov's orchestration. But unlike other composers who sought an 'authentic' version of nationalism by adopting a more ethnographic approach, Prokofiev fashioned his own musical language, inspired and connected to music he was immersed in from an early age. Prokofiev's preference, for example, was always to use Russian sources in his operas, in his musical works set both before he left Imperial Russia and when he returned to the Soviet Union. His unparalleled setting of the Russian language, such as in his opera *The Gambler*, surpassed the declamatory experiments of Alexander Dargomyzhsky; his work was the natural progression of Modest Mussorgsky's. Combined with his interest in the development of Russian theatre, such as that of the director Vsevolod Meyerhold, he was able to challenge the realistic approach to opera as drama, where he abandoned set-pieces like arias and ensembles to allow the drama to unfold as part of a structure that he preferred to call 'theatrical rhythm'.[6] He constantly appraised the work of Russian composers working in the domain of Russian music. Much about Prokofiev's personal artistry and musical identity has been overshadowed by the geopolitical decisions he made. The time has come for us to cast aside these traditional narratives and to fully probe this musical giant's aesthetics and artistic inclinations. He is now firmly established as a classic of the twentieth century – a position that would have satisfied him no end – and yet there is much to learn about his musical and artistic constitution.

For a biography of this nature to be valuable, we must, however, contextualize Prokofiev beyond simply observing a geographical location and evaluating the works he happened to be working on at the time. Rather we must look at the way he chose to continue to interact with Russia, and later the Soviet Union, with the information and lived experience he had to hand, despite the challenges that he faced while abroad and on his return. Even as we acknowledge the critical role self-identifying as Russian assumed in the composer's complex identity, we must simultaneously consider how he belonged to several worlds – some conflicting and some complementary. He found navigating in and out of these worlds difficult and somewhat hypocritical at the best of times. Over time the pressure of being pulled in different directions accumulated and weighed heavily on him. This put a strain on his romantic and professional relationships, his friendships and later on his marriage. The scars and challenges of marriage were the deepest and most complex, because unlike the composer, his first wife Lina was at ease with her cosmopolitan identity. Ultimately Prokofiev remained wary of possible contamination, as he saw it, should he be too aesthetically influenced by a cosmopolitan way of thinking. This attitude is particularly evident in his late years abroad when he was largely based in Paris and writing works like *Le Pas d'Acier* and *Prodigal Son*. His preference for relying on his own musical instincts rather than working closely with other artists, like the Ukrainian choreographer Serge Lifar, strained his collaborative relationships in these years.

Crucially, this biography aims to look at Prokofiev through an additional, alternative lens to those which biographical studies have offered us so far. Here the composer is positioned as a cosmopolitan caught between cataclysmic events and the global mobilization of people around 1917. Throughout his life, Prokofiev struggled with the identities assigned to him, and detested being categorized as an émigré.[7] Although he found temporary respite in émigré circles in Paris, he was far from feeling at home there. On a personal level, he never accepted the label of Russian émigré, but he possibly conceived of himself as a Soviet citizen even less. Although he may have had a comfortable early upbringing, he had to fend for himself following his graduation and carve out a sustainable artistic career, like many others. As a result of global events, starting with the Russian Revolution in 1917, he spent most of his first decade abroad on the move, trying to survive. All the while he stayed true to artistic ideals that remained surprisingly constant despite the harrowing conditions he was forced to work in for the last fifteen years of his life. Central to this positioning of Prokofiev is his artistic trajectory, from his initial experimentation as composer–pianist to his posthumous emergence as a classic of the twentieth century and beyond.

Both in Europe and in Russia, the years before the First World War were characterized by swiftly changing political and artistic currents. The continent was politically charged and unstable: new powers challenged old; empires were poised to tumble. Discontent, uprisings, assassinations, terrorism and – eventually – revolution typified the turn of the century and the following decades in Russia. Unlike Igor Stravinsky, Prokofiev did not have a safety network of family ties or strong finances to cushion the blow, should he have failed to make a living for himself. Although he entered the spotlight only five years or so after Stravinsky (Prokofiev always liked to remind Stravinsky that he was nine years younger than him), it might as well have been a decade or two later, such were the calamitous changes fuelling this period. Parallels with Stravinsky, although inevitable, do not illuminate the very different set of circumstances Prokofiev was working in. Prokofiev had some links with influential figures, such as Sergei Diaghilev, but this was not enough to secure the sustainable career he needed. The younger Russian had no choice but to start from scratch. To the outside world of course, the similarities between Stravinsky and Prokofiev would have far outweighed the differences. Both were Russians who left their country prior to the revolution; both were intimately connected with St Petersburg Conservatory and both were exiles who chose to live in Paris, for a time at least. Both worked with Diaghilev and the Ballets Russes; they were friends and they moved in similar circles. But the differences in their conditions should not be underestimated.

In truth Prokofiev was part of the establishment far more than he would ever care to admit, and certainly more than Stravinsky was; not just because he was a graduate of the St Petersburg Conservatory but because there was never any doubt as to his calling. We will also see how, despite his reputation as an enfant terrible, he desired the approval of the musical establishment. Prokofiev never saw any other career paths (such as law, which both Stravinsky and Diaghilev flirted with) as options. He was acquainted with Stravinsky's work early on but also felt superior to the older composer, for reasons that will become gradually apparent as we progress through his life story. Prokofiev was also a prize-winning pianist, with a successful performing career from his early years, which Stravinsky was not. Indeed, he mocked Stravinsky when the latter started to practise to be able to play his own works, clearly forgetting how many hours he himself had needed to put in during his conservatory days to master the instrument.

Stravinsky's relationship with Diaghilev came earlier than Prokofiev's and was on a strong footing. In contrast, the younger composer's entry into the Ballets Russes coterie happened in fits and starts. The two composers also had different perspectives on the political events unfolding in Russia. Stravinsky had no patience for post-revolutionary Russia. He had no desire to kindle friendships or to accept any offers of reconciliation. He refused all openings and invitations from the Bolsheviks and later the Communists to return, firmly putting Russia behind him. Instead, he looked first to 'old' Europe and then to America for inspiration. Prokofiev, on the other hand, kept his Russian friends close and his options open. He had always had a strong artistic following in Russia, and Russian enthusiasm and support did not dampen during his years abroad. Rather, his audience there waited patiently and hopefully for a homecoming.

Prokofiev then, like so many others, was a cultural and artistic exile. In retrospect and with hindsight it might seem that he was unwittingly caught in the global movement of people. It was customary for Russian artists to make a name for themselves overseas and then return home, but the irretrievable gulf only became obvious to him once he was in the United States and receiving reports from afar of the progress of the revolution. At that point he understood that he was trapped outside Russia, although he could not imagine how long for. From then on, the yearning to go back was never far from his mind, but with other important events overtaking his life, he had to bide his time. The 'whiff of the past', as he called it, held sway over Prokofiev and he returned to this theme at various points in his life. In his rational and considered way he continued to ponder this pull: 'is it because the Revolution has erected such a barrier between me and the past? Or is it that life abroad, far away from Russia, has proved such a strong desire to recall all that is Russian?'[8] Edward Said has characterized exile as 'the unhealable rift forced between a human being and a native place'.[9] Prokofiev struggled with this rift to the extent that the lure of the return home gradually overtook all other considerations. The composer was adamant throughout his life (this is evident in his diaries, letters and different forms of personal correspondence) that he was not an émigré. In other words, he actively chose not to completely sever his ties with his homeland in the way that Igor Stravinsky, Sergei Rachmaninov and Nikolai Medtner did.

For contemporary Western audiences, Prokofiev's sound, harmonies, melodic turns of phrase and intervallic nuances, even his compositional techniques, sounded undoubtedly Russian.[10] One might argue that for Westerners the sound of his music and his harmonies remains distinctively Russian, although it continues to be an almost futile endeavour to identify the features that make it so. However, for Prokofiev, as we shall see, the concept of a Russian element in his music is no more or less important than other strands that contribute to his uniqueness as a composer, a singularity that is characterized by his uncompromising and distinctive approach to musical aesthetics. But what conceptualizations of Russia in sound, art and literature meant to Prokofiev at different points in his life is an essential question that underlies our present narrative. Indeed, we could argue that the composer – at least in the first decade or so of his career – was very much anti-establishment rather than necessarily anti-tradition. He had no compelling desire to work within one cultural tradition as opposed to another, but prized his own originality, particularly melodic, above all things. His blueprint for composing music that remains so popular to this very day was entirely his own. How melodic material is worked through in his compositions tells us a great deal about his aesthetic ideals as his career developed. Scholars like Marina Raku have recently commented on Prokofiev's appreciation of the theory of tonal relationship. This comprised modulation that took place between keys that overlapped tonally or at least had common elements, which included specific intervals and chords. The technique of modulation is an endlessly intriguing one in Prokofiev's music – it is linked to his understanding of musical narrative and his relationship with the listener. Most importantly, however, he understood the trends and traditions of his day, including those of Rimsky-Korsakov, Sergei Taneyev and Alexander Scriabin, but had distinctive and clear ideas about how he intended to deviate from such customs.[11]

As already indicated, the underlying scope here is to fully explore the composer's originality, to uncover his sources of inspiration – some of which might be quite surprising – as well as to consider his appropriation and reconfiguration of 'Russian' materials across all 'periods' of his life. We will look at Prokofiev the artist, the composer and the pianist, and observe the ways in which he negotiated these identities while fraught with instability and anxiety brought about by exile. We will also consider Prokofiev's pianist/performer persona – he curated this identity with great care, and it was how he initially interacted with audiences. Understanding this persona and how it came into being is key to understanding who he was and why he might want to go back to his homeland. It helps us obtain a sense of his conservatory and post-conservatory days, the circles he moved in and what motivated the development of his aesthetics. His early memories of St Petersburg and Russia in general were joyful and carefree, and the pull of these early days was strong, providing a nostalgic refrain through his life. He would always consider these years as creatively rich, energetic and innovative, and he would yearn for those years of creative unrestraint long after that freedom had dissipated forever beyond his reach. Above all things, he was essentially a forward-focused optimist. This comes across in his diary, which the present biography will refer to in depth, in his letters and – most clearly – in his music.

Current scholarship from across the East–West divide has concerned itself with how Prokofiev was perceived as an exile, especially when considered alongside Stravinsky, Rachmaninov, Medtner and others. But these narratives are almost always tinged with an element of prejudgement angled at proving why or how the desire for Prokofiev's return home took root with a much less nuanced discussion of his works or musical aesthetics. Through an overview of key themes emerging from the reception of his music as well his performances, we shall see how the composer did not interact well with 'isms' – not because he was afraid of not fitting in, or even, as has been occasionally suggested, because he didn't understand them, but because he believed in being true only to his own artistry. Aspects of modernism in his work will be problematized and explored alongside his preferred compositional and artistic models of Scriabin and Mussorgsky.[12] In Britain, whose

audiences and artists Prokofiev deeply respected, the composer
was often perplexed by the reactions he provoked. Despite such
repeated misunderstandings, British audiences – at least during
the composer's lifetime – were only exposed to small portions of
his work and were thus unable to evaluate it accurately or to place it
within the broader context of his compositional ideas and musical
pathways. Critical perception of Prokofiev's music in the Anglo-
American world changed gradually during the composer's lifetime
and over the two decades that the composer himself graced these
international stages. It is only very recently, with the appearance of
the composer's own diaries, revisionist biographies of the composer
and with new research coming to light, that Prokofiev's music is
now being evaluated more comprehensively.[13] Narratives about
his life, ideas and aesthetics can now attain a balance hitherto
unavailable to us.

In this biography we will see Prokofiev emerge as an
international artist who gave concerts to various audiences, but
who initially struggled to make ends meet. As he grew from his
experiences, he became better able to determine and command
his own worth. The composer was a man of many faces and,
perhaps unsurprisingly, his years abroad were unstable, often full
of anxiety and worry. Like many other artists, he settled in Paris
for a large part of these years: he lived with his wife and children
in France and often spent summers in other parts of Europe
visiting friends and reconnecting with acquaintances from his
early years in St Petersburg. In his first years after leaving Russia,
which turned out to be years of exile, Prokofiev had to think on
his feet and tap into his entrepreneurial mindset, promote his
works and liaise with conductors and key people who could help
secure performances. He chased his own contracts and scrutinized
the legal and financial terms – with, at times, great difficulty: we
can see this in his letters to the Chicago Opera and the German
opera houses, who were at various times preparing to stage his
works. It is easy to see how frustrating this could have been for a
less resilient character than Prokofiev. The evidence now available
shows that he was often treated like an itinerant and naive artist. It

was clear too that contractors, managers and so on were trying to take advantage of him, and, in his view, were devaluing his work. He fought, aggressively even, for performance rights to his works and strove to obtain concert contracts that lasted from three to five years to create a sense of security for himself (and soon after for his family). A lesser artist than Prokofiev would have been disheartened long before. Instead, he relied on his instincts and on his entrepreneurship, driven by an intrinsic and unshakeable belief in his own worth and that of his music.[14]

For several years, Prokofiev's life was one without any financial security, where he was on the move from one engagement to another, struggling with the melancholy of his peripatetic lifestyle. He often had to battle with prejudice and occasionally with xenophobia (even if, as we shall see from contemporary press reception, this was politically motivated). This biography situates Prokofiev as an artistic exile first and foremost, and it is through this lens that I hope to demonstrate how his life was in many ways exceptional and extraordinary. It was a feat of survival and perseverance. There are many excellent biographies of Prokofiev that reflect and consider new archival discoveries situating his return to the Soviet Union within the political circumstances of the time. The present narrative instead seeks to demonstrate how Prokofiev responded to the times that he was living in, and how he constantly tried to place musical and artistic life at the centre of all his endeavours.

To write about Prokofiev chronologically is no easy task. One could of course choose to follow the path of his geographical location, but it would soon become evident that there was a clear lag between his physical and cultural location and his compositional outputs. This delay is obvious when one considers that his pre-revolutionary works, like *Chout* and *The Gambler,* were premiered five and ten years after they were composed respectively.[15] To Prokofiev's mind, these works were of the moment when they were written, but by the time they were premiered, the composer, and often the world around him, had moved on aesthetically. If we are to trace the list of works as they were composed, we might see the logic behind the musical works, but at the expense of the composer's interactions with his lived present. In the present text, I have chosen to tread a precarious path and weave a way around both: the chronology is preserved as far as possible but not at the expense of us understanding why Prokofiev made the decisions that he did – decisions which might have been driven by anything from aesthetics and style to personal and business matters. Like the endearing side-step in his harmony or the quirks in some of his melodic motifs and rhythms, Prokofiev's life was almost always lived betwixt the musical chromatic steps and the rhythmic off-beat.

Much has been said about Prokofiev's 'periods', his Soviet travails often being compared and contrasted – favourably or unfavourably, depending on the lens of appraisal – with his years in the West. The assignation of three stages or chapters to his life – partitioning it neatly into his early life in Russia, his time spent abroad and his return to the Soviet Union – confirms and situates him alongside the 'great' composers described in the textbooks of music history. The lure of the prodigal myth, laid out as it is in the tripartite story of his life, is strong and not one that Soviet musicologists, critics and politicians could ignore. His 'return' was a great coup for the Soviet regime, publicized and vaunted as approval for their cultural reforms. But what of Prokofiev? What did the man himself think of his life and legacy? Did he see himself as Russia's prodigal son? Investigating this might provide some clues to his reasoning and decision-making processes, which have often been critiqued as callous and calculated by some and misguided and selfish by others.

On his return to the Soviet Union, a move many of his friends considered unwise, Prokofiev focused on the connections between his own understanding of composition and its role in society and that of the new Soviet state. Of course, it was only once he was fully installed within the infrastructures and the cultural web of the Soviet Union that he realized there was an enormous gulf between the value he placed on musical and artistic independence and how much innovation was permitted in practice. To the regime, and to all intents and purposes to wider Soviet society, Prokofiev was an outsider. He could not even begin to understand the harsher reality that Dmitri Shostakovich and many others inhabited and struggled with daily. He may not have felt like a stranger; indeed, he considered himself more at home in the Soviet Union than in any other place he had lived in the previous decade, but there would be consequences to his initial immunity from criticism. Despite the best attempts of his close friend Nikolai Myaskovsky, who tried to explain some of the complexities underpinning the real situation to him, he would not come to know, understand and experience the severe consequences associated with independent artistic thought until a decade later. Because he was a new acquisition for the Soviet government, Prokofiev did not face any long-lasting humiliations until 1948. He was largely materially unaffected by the infamously venomous *Pravda* article of 1936 that condemned Shostakovich's *Lady Macbeth*. It is hard to imagine that he would not have given this debacle grave consideration in his own private way; ultimately, he most likely thought that what had happened to Shostakovich, a younger composer more intertwined with the Soviet cultural world than he ever was, could never possibly happen to him. And for a long while, it didn't.

1

The Road to Petersburg

In essence, I am the student of my own ideas.
Sergei Prokofiev[1]

From his early composing days, Prokofiev was cautious of influence, preferring to rely on his own methods, often beautifully idiosyncratic, of solving musical problems. This is evident in the way he handles form and structure, his ideas for the operatic and musical stage, his compositional methods such as his reworking of musical materials, and his harmonic landscapes and modulation preferences, for example. This is not to say that he was immune to influence, but rather that these influences came from unexpected sources. Early on, he found inspiration in Alexander Scriabin and Richard Strauss; later one can hear echoes of Igor Stravinsky and Pyotr Ilyich Tchaikovsky. Having found a secure musical voice, Prokofiev rejected many contemporary trends; he avoided experimentation for its own sake and continued to believe in his own distinctive soundworlds. He harboured these convictions through his life, including after his return to the USSR.

The story of Prokofiev begins well over a hundred years ago. His childhood years and juvenilia are not unique but they demonstrate how Prokofiev's prodigious gift developed and was in turn nurtured by those around him in the early years. These years reveal qualities about him, both human and artistic, that were forged in the early years, and that continued to motivate his later focus in life. The composer conceived of himself, quite rightly as it transpired, as a unique artist with a powerful and independent artistic voice;

a man with a path all of his own making and quite different from that of his contemporaries. It is hard for historians of music to situate Prokofiev. His sound is distinctive: he does not easily fit into music history textbooks, and his music crosses genres and experiments across artistic boundaries (something especially evident in his later years). A Prokofiev bassline is recognizable immediately, as is one of his exquisite long-limbed melodies. These qualities make this giant of the twentieth century hard to categorize formally and systematically, and to do so would be a fruitless endeavour. Rather, let us take an intense look at the artist as a young man because it was in his early years that his artistic temperament was nurtured and forged. Repeatedly, in testing times, Prokofiev would hold on to the ideals and philosophical approaches of his pre- and post-revolutionary years. For that reason alone, our first focus must be these early years until around 1916, which will help us understand how Prokofiev thought of himself as 'Russian' and how he, rather than anyone else, conceived this. Comparisons with Stravinsky and Shostakovich, though common, can be both unhelpful and misleading.

Prokofiev was born in Sontsivka, in Ukraine's Donetsk Oblast, in 1891. He was the only child of Mariya Grigoryevna Prokofiev (née Zhitkova) and Sergei Alexandrovich Prokofiev. Two sisters had died before him, so it is unsurprising that he had the full attention and devotion of his mother. His father was an agricultural engineer and managed the Sontsivka estate. Prokofiev learnt Russian, arithmetic, geography and history with his father. His mother was a strong-minded and intelligent woman who graduated from a lyceum (institute of higher learning) with a gold medal award. In Sontsivka she had the run of a large estate and had to support Sergei Alexandrovich in the management of it, a role she relished. By all accounts Prokofiev's mother was a curious, intelligent and well-read person. She was a sophisticated woman who took every opportunity to visit cities and their cultural institutions, and she took her young, inquisitive son with her when she could. She was an excellent pianist as well as a philanthropist.

Mariya Grigoryevna practised the piano every day. As a hugely talented, if amateur, pianist she had three musical virtues:

'persistence, love, and taste'.[2] She allowed the young Prokofiev to explore the sounds and shapes of music, for example by experimenting with rhythmic shapes, melodic fragments and registers. The juvenilia from this period are illuminating in this regard.[3] Prokofiev describes his mother fondly in his memoir and remembers that, above all, her approach to teaching him music was to allow his creativity free rein. The downside of such a broad-minded teaching approach was that he did not learn pieces properly and was not taught how to position his hands (and feet) at the piano; as he puts it, his 'thoughts would run ahead, and my fingers would follow somehow or other'.[4] Swiftly, he learnt to notate music under the tutelage of his mother, who strived 'to make things interesting, to expand my horizons, to develop skills gradually, and above all not to alienate me with drudgery'.[5] Prokofiev would spend time working on these less appealing technical and performance skills when he joined the conservatory.

As is to be expected, Mariya Grigoryevna was an influential figure in Prokofiev's life – she doted on him, nurtured his musical talent and supported his fledgling career. Her natural instincts were always to protect Prokofiev and to foster in him a sense of awareness of his own individuality.[6] This endowed him with an unshakeable belief and self-confidence that would remain with him for the rest of his life. Prokofiev attended church with his mother, where he heard vespers sung on liturgical holidays. He therefore grew up in a loving but intense, incubated environment; surrounded by books and music, working under the close eye of his mother and his French governess, his early childhood was structured around his development. He soon began to show an interest in playing and writing his own pieces of music. The sounds that he heard in his childhood home remained with him all his life and can be found as traces in his music across all periods and styles of writing.

As a child growing up in Sontsivka he listened to the music of Ludwig van Beethoven, Frédéric Chopin, Franz Liszt, Tchaikovsky and Anton Rubinstein.[7] He often sat by his mother while she was practising, picking out tunes and short motifs on the piano. Prokofiev appears to have enjoyed improvising, a practice he did not take with him into adulthood, noting in an entry from 1913 that he 'never discovered any useful material for my compositions by means of improvising'.[8] In his autobiography, the composer also notes that he would transpose pieces in different keys, trying to find the one that sounded best. He went through enormous amounts of repertoire, becoming a skilled sight-reader in the process. His mother continued to foster this critical independence, urging him to discuss the pieces he was playing.

Prokofiev developed relatively early as a composer and started writing music for the piano well before he had himself approached full technical mastery of the instrument; this is especially obvious during his time at the conservatory (1904–13) when he was writing works and concurrently practising intensively to prepare them for performance. The *Toccata*, op. 11, is the most obvious example. In these early experimental, largely self-taught days, piano playing for Prokofiev was often a case of making his fingers catch up to the musical ideas in his imagination and finding creative, if not always pianistic, ways of achieving the sounds he desired. The piano functioned as a sounding board for ideas and themes explored mentally before they were written down and transcribed for the piano. It also meant that his fingers were at the service of his ideas; his idiosyncratic way of playing the piano was rooted in his early need to use the instrument as a testing ground.

Prokofiev's pre-conservatory output is of two kinds: compositions for piano and those for the theatre. On the one hand, the former are almost an exercise in musical and pianistic discipline – in composing for the piano, he wrote for the only instrument and soundscape that he was, as yet, familiar with. On the other hand, the latter allowed him more freedom to experiment with various sound combinations, effects and structures. The fantastic became crucial to Prokofiev's understanding of the concept of theatricality, and its integration into his compositional style is particularly evident in his operas.[9] It emerged in the juvenile operas, for example in *The Giant and Undina*, and was then developed in his later works: *Maddalena, The Gambler, The Love for Three Oranges* and *Fiery Angel*. All these later operas use the fantastic, albeit in various ways and to different extents. Prokofiev's version of the fantastic in his stage works has much to do with extravagance, the absurd and the grotesque, but it also plays upon the 'quaint' aspect of the term. *Fiery Angel* is a prime example of extravagance and the grotesque but *The Gambler* and *The Love for Three Oranges* are the composer's subtler take on the fantastic: they play upon the 'eccentric' but also on the 'imaginary' nuances of the definition.

In January 1902 Prokofiev accompanied his mother to Moscow, where she had arranged for her son to meet the venerable composer and teacher Sergei Taneyev. This introduction was secured through a family friend, Yury Pomerantsev, who was himself studying at the Moscow Conservatory. Taneyev was impressed by the young Prokofiev, noting in his diary that the boy had 'outstanding talent . . . he played his compositions [and had] absolute pitch, he recognise[d] intervals, chords'.[10] Taneyev recommended that Prokofiev take lessons with Pomerantsev, insisting on the 'correct instruction of harmony' to prevent bad habits settling in.[11] Pomerantsev gave Prokofiev a few lessons, explaining four-voice counterpoint and setting him assignments in harmony, but the young composer bristled at what he thought were pointless exercises, noting in his autobiography that he 'wanted to compose operas with marches, storms and complicated scenes'.[12]

Eventually Taneyev recommended that Prokofiev spend a summer studying music with a former pupil of his, Reinhold Glière. The younger composer took charge of Prokofiev's piano-playing, starting him off with Beethoven's sonatas. He also introduced him to a great deal of new repertoire and used the sonatas to explain elements of form. Curiously, under Glière's guidance, Prokofiev's piano-playing improved to such an extent that his mother stopped playing altogether.[13] Perhaps she felt awed by her own son's prodigious talents, or perhaps she didn't want to compel him to listen to her playing when he was exposed to elite performances at the conservatory. Glière also taught his pupil how to write in four-part phrases and how to modulate, additionally explaining the song form to him, which Prokofiev then proceeded to work with in his first set of 'Little Songs', as he called them. In these pieces, Glière instructed Prokofiev to create variations upon the basic elements that he had taught him until he was satisfied that his student had mastered the song form. After that, they moved on to orchestration, with Prokofiev deciding to orchestrate the storm music (which does not survive) from his opera *On Desert Islands.* Following this, the ambitious young composer wanted to write a symphony, and while Glière thought it was too soon for the exercise, he eventually acquiesced to the persistent young man.

Mariya Grigoryevna explored options for her son's music education in both Moscow and St Petersburg, and finally, after extensive discussions with her husband, as well as with Alexander Glazunov, the principal of the St Petersburg Conservatory, the Prokofievs settled on the latter city. Prokofiev's entrance into the conservatory in 1904, at the age of thirteen, marked a new stage in his awareness of himself both as a composer and, perhaps more importantly, as a pianist.[14] As one of the youngest students at the conservatory, he understandably found it hard to make friends, although he had good enough relationships with Nikolai Myaskovsky and Boris Zakharov. The former became Prokofiev's most trusted and respected friend – the only other composer with whom he felt comfortable sharing musical ideas, drafts and sketches. It was a friendship that would last a lifetime and would provide him with a continuous connection to his homeland, even during his time abroad.

Despite the bravado Prokofiev expressed in his diaries and his autobiography, one can only imagine how challenging this context would have been for an impressionable teenager. Uprooted from everything he knew and loved in Sontsivka, Prokofiev moved with his mother to St Petersburg, where she had relatives, the Raevskys. They rented a modest apartment at 90 Sadovaya Street and Mariya Grigoryevna dedicated herself to making their life pleasant, ensuring her son had every material comfort that he needed to succeed in his studies. They had a circle of friends and immersed themselves in city life with great gusto. The Raevskys introduced Prokofiev to high society with its manners and peculiarities; his mother even paid for dancing lessons, not that he would ever learn to avoid stepping on his partner's toes! Prokofiev missed his father a great deal and kept up a regular correspondence with him. In his letters to his father he is opinionated, pronouncing Tchaikovsky's *Queen of Spades* to be a good opera, albeit with 'revolting' singing and stage sets. Early on, and thanks to his mother's encouragement, Prokofiev kept diaries, which on reading today demonstrate his sharp and sardonic wit, his meticulousness as well as a variety of interests, including tennis and chess.

Prokofiev was a student at the conservatory at a critical time in Imperial Russia. He studied with influential teachers, some of whom, like the eminent Nikolai Rimsky-Korsakov, would shape the future of Russian music. His other teachers included Anatoly Lyadov, Nikolai Tcherepnin and Alexander Glazunov, all venerable figures that, to Prokofiev's mind at least, represented a version of academicism in music that he was not interested in. At the St Petersburg Conservatory, as Marina Raku has explained, young composers were immersed in the ideology of the Mighty Handful, also known as 'the Five', even if the programme taught within the institution was strongly academic with a good grounding in Western compositional techniques. The composers of the Mighty Handful – Rimsky-Korsakov, Mily Balakirev, César Cui, Modest Mussorgsky and Alexander Borodin – shared the aim of creating a specifically national style of Russian music. Prokofiev's professors all subscribed to these ideals even if they were not necessarily teaching the Five's compositions in the core curriculum.[15] Quite typically, Prokofiev initially resisted these ideas about nationalism in Russian music and calls for a specific Russian style. In his early works especially, he was highly critical of these ideals, purposely looking for new and unique ways of expressing his innate ideas, which did not immediately endear him to his teachers.[16] Vera Alpers, a peer of Prokofiev's, provides some amusing insights into the 'dignified', neatly dressed blonde boy with lively eyes.[17] He was very advanced in general education subjects, which his father had home-schooled him in, and he kept a detailed report on the achievements of other students, including writing out statistical tables with records of marks, a predilection which irritated other students no end.

Prokofiev's first piano teacher at the conservatory was Alexander Winkler and he studied solfeggio and harmony with Anatoly Lyadov, whose classes he abhorred for their dry nature and mostly disengaged professor.[18] The youthful composer, like many other students, thought Lyadov was a dour and peevish teacher. However, what Prokofiev learned in these lessons remained with him his entire life. Lyadov schooled the irreverent young man in harmony and was a stickler for rules of form and traditional counterpoint. Unsurprisingly the young iconoclast could not see the relevance of what he was being taught to his own compositional ideals. But one might argue that Prokofiev did owe Lyadov a great deal; the thorough grounding in the rules of harmony and counterpoint gave him the freedom to flout musical conventions to create the sound we have come to associate with his music. An older Prokofiev reflected that he had 'made no attempt to apply what I had learned in harmony class to my composing. On the contrary, while composing I strove to get away from all that – which was roughly the same thing I had done two years before.'[19] Displaying a stubborn streak and a consistent belief in the wisdom of his own approach, Prokofiev maintained this opposition between his conventional harmony classes and his own (until then largely private) practice of composing. His desire for innovation not just in terms of harmony but in the practice of composition more generally is evident as early as 1902, but the conservatory period only served to strengthen his resolve to be innovative and individual in his writing.

Prokofiev initially found Winkler to be a good piano teacher, although he did not particularly enjoy his discipline and attention to detail. Indeed, like any impatient and talented student he complained that

> for some two weeks I would have to play only exercises aimed to strengthen the fingers and to develop the wrist . . . until then I played everything but did it rather carelessly, holding my fingers straight, like sticks. Winkler insisted on my playing accurately, holding my fingers in the rounded shape and putting them down with precision.[20]

The focused hard work paid off. Four years later, he modestly observed that he had 'abilities as a pianist'.[21] But he could not seem to rid himself of his 'most peculiar way of arranging his legs under the piano'.[22] The move from Winkler's piano class to Anna Esipova's was a critical event in Prokofiev's development as a concert pianist.[23] By this point, he was both unhappy and uninspired by his piano lessons with Winkler. There was, as he recalls, an 'unbridgeable gulf in understanding' between them and, as time went on, it seemed to Prokofiev that Winkler repeated himself and did not provide any new insights. Around this time, the young composer had begun to think that a performing career as a concert pianist was a viable option. 'What is the point of my sitting for another two or three years to stay effectively in the same place, when I feel that I have great potential for the piano and my ambition is to be a good pianist?'[24] He made the decision to focus on concertizing late in his conservatory career, at least in comparison to Rachmaninov and Scriabin. Prokofiev would always consider Rachmaninov the superior pianist, referring to his pianism (as opposed to his compositions) as a source of inspiration. When preparing his Piano Concerto No. 2 for performance in 1924, he wryly noted that he was not allowing 'a single doubtful note. If I keep this up I shall be able to match Rachmaninoff for impeccability.'[25]

His mind made up, Prokofiev approached Esipova through a friend of his, Boris Zakharov, who was one of her students, and joined her class at the conservatory in June 1909. He spent the summer working on the classics – Bach, Handel, Mozart, Beethoven – as she requested him to do in preparation for the next conservatory year. Esipova advised her students to work on scales, chords and arpeggios, thirds and octaves as well as ornaments. She taught them to work on precise legato and staccato articulation, to cultivate a cantilena touch and to pay careful attention to dynamics and pedalling. These were all qualities that would be useful to the aspiring concert pianist, but although he focused on improving his technique, Esipova remained unsatisfied with his cantilena line – in other words, his abilty to project melodic lines. Nonetheless, despite the erratic practice and his selective acceptance and application of

Anna Esipova at the piano, date unknown.

Esipova's teaching methods, Prokofiev seemed to have acquired new inspiration to work. Making a move to change his piano teacher proved to be an invaluable step forward for him.

Esipova's class rejuvenated Prokofiev and forced him to reconsider his career priorities. All her students wanted to become piano virtuosos and their piano playing was at an extraordinarily high level: her students were generally regarded as the best pianists in the conservatory. For a composer prone to keeping his eyes on his surroundings as well as being intensely focused on his career, Prokofiev notes that 'the high point began from the day I returned to St Petersburg, with my initiation into Esipova's class, the success of my studies with a marvellous new professor who motivated me to work with enthusiasm.'[26] He responded to this challenge in kind by taking the 'greatest pains' in preparing for his lessons.[27] Esipova addressed the issues he continued to experience with hand positioning. She insisted he play with curved fingers, something that arguably, from later pictures we have of Prokofiev's hand positions on the piano, he never quite mastered. She also worked with him on his pedalling, which 'caused her to cry out in dismay'.[28]

Esipova made critical comments on his performance of his own music, which he documented meticulously and dispassionately in his diaries: 'It's all very well to have accents, but you mustn't play fortissimo all the time. And you constantly overpedal.'[29] His problem with posture came to the fore in his conducting attempts. His conducting teacher, Nikolai Tcherepnin, critiqued his 'frightful gestures' and 'contorted body'.[30] This made him ever more aware of his own image, his physique and bodily gestures. He began to practise conducting in front of a mirror with a view to ameliorating the fluidity of his gestures. Over time he observed, with some pleasure, his improved fluidity of movement.

Coinciding with his burgeoning performing career, which – like any working musician – Prokofiev developed outside conservatory hours and curricula, his repertoire changed to become more mainstream, in keeping with the traditional concert pianist's route. With Esipova he studied Bach's fugues, Beethoven and Mozart's sonatas, Chopin's Piano Sonata No. 2 and polonaises, Liszt's B minor Sonata, 'Feux Follets' and *Tannhäuser* transcription, Schumann's *Toccata* and Piano Sonata No. 1 in F-sharp minor and Tchaikovsky's Piano Concerto No. 1.[31] An intense fascination with the pianistic virtuoso tradition and a passion for Liszt characterize this period. But crucially, Prokofiev intended to engage with the concept of virtuosity in a personal way. Not content with becoming a pianist, like any other in Esipova's class, virtuosity now became a site of

Sergei Prokofiev, wearing a dark, military-style jacket, seated with Dr Alfred Reberg's daughters, Vera, Zina and Nina, Sontsivka, *c.* 1909. Dr Reberg was the Prokofievs' family doctor.

negotiation between his individual playing technique and that of the Romantic tradition of which his highly esteemed teacher was a representative. This iconoclastic re-envisioning of virtuosity is evident in the pieces he composed during this period, such as the two collections of pieces for piano, op. 3 and op. 4, which include his early signature performing piece, *Diabolical Suggestion*. This short but dramatic piece personifies him (as pianist) and his music in this period.

By 1913, however, an increasingly confident Prokofiev had outgrown his enthusiasm for Esipova's teaching and indeed for the establishment more generally, which he had never thought too highly of anyway. He felt very strongly that he was ready to independently embark on his own career. His most telling indictment of Esipova comes in a diary entry from that year, in which he acerbically, and certainly unfairly, concludes that 'overall Esipova had done me more harm than good, putting me off performing on stage and taking away from me much of my love for and joy in the instrument.'[32] It is fortuitous that Prokofiev came to this realization towards the end of his piano studies at the conservatory. As he was about to immerse himself in preparing for the final exam in piano, he was too busy to get into the innumerable arguments with Esipova that would otherwise no doubt have ensued; the composer was not one to shy away from confrontation.

Despite his years under Esipova's watchful eye, Prokofiev stubbornly retained, and even curated, a unique performing style, with gestures that dated back to his early days of piano-playing – when playing was a game or sport rather than a means to define himself. Claude Debussy heard a young Prokofiev play in St Petersburg in November 1913, when the latter performed his Étude no. 3 and *Legenda* and remarked upon 'the individuality of [Prokofiev's] technique'.[33] Perhaps Debussy was in a position where he felt he needed to make some observation on Prokofiev's playing, or perhaps it was a genuine comment, but an instinctive approach to piano-playing still characterized his performances and indeed drove his compositions for piano in the first decade of his career. The constituent elements of Prokofiev's performing style were a unique balance of technique, rhythmic drive, manipulation of touch with theatricality and a selection of narrative devices. Prokofiev's enthusiasm for the instrument is infectious and reflects his passion for taking centre stage. Some of his observations deserve a longer quote:

> I love to see a grand piano with the lid open, in position on the stage in front of the orchestra, ready for the concert. The thought came to me that in the course of my life I should no doubt be both playing and conducting a great many concerts. Which of these activities would I be doing more often, it would be interesting to know?![34]

Prokofiev drew critical attention to his compositions when he played them himself. This was crucial to his artistry and development as a musician. His first compositions were very obviously written for him to play – his idiosyncrasies, physical preferences and strengths were written into the music. His onstage theatrical style then transformed those early pieces, such as the op. 4 and the *Sarcasms,* op. 17, into musical events. These works were written in quick succession and over a short period of time; a highly energized Prokofiev was inspired by the possibilities emerging from playing and was, perhaps quite narcissistically, drawn to his own musical problem-solving. Some of these pieces, which he would play on his first tours of the West, were initially indecipherable to audiences. The agogic accents, the rhythmic energy, the technically demanding passages in thirds and octaves, the sheer physical strength needed to play this early piano music testifies to the fact that not only was Prokofiev writing his own strengths into the pieces, but, as yet anyway, he was the only one who could do them justice in performance. The composer, conductor and erstwhile Glière student Alexander Yurasovsky, an acquaintance of Prokofiev, intimated this after hearing the composer play his second piano sonata; he observed that 'while of course it was very interesting and inventive, it had not a scrap of real melody in it, just a series of "tigerish leaps".'[35] The physical dimension of his playing and his integration of various bodily gestures into the score were inseparable from his performing style.

Having drawn the attention of St Petersburg's intellectual avant-garde, who were constantly on alert for the latest innovation, in February 1908, around the time he was moving from Winkler to Esipova, Prokofiev was invited to audition for the organizing committee of Evenings of Contemporary Music.[36] The society was loosely affiliated with Sergei Diaghilev's movement and magazine *Mir iskusstva,* which was then a hotbed of contemporary musical trends. The society also invited composers from abroad to attend their musical soirées and mingle with the local musical figures. Relationships were made and critical introductions brokered. Music by Arnold Schoenberg, Gustav Mahler, Richard Strauss, Max Reger, Claude Debussy and Maurice Ravel (among others) was performed. The evenings aimed to support local talent, provided it was innovative and iconoclastic. Prokofiev's early music, for instance, was played alongside that of Stravinsky and Myaskovsky. His introduction to the society played an important part in widening his knowledge of modernist repertoire and, most importantly, in developing his entrepreneurial instincts. His shorter piano pieces, which he naturally played himself, met with success. The audience at these performances included some of the most unorthodox and uncompromising aesthetic thinkers critical to the lifeblood of St Petersburg's contemporary cultural scene, such as Alfred Nurok, Walter Nouvel, Alexander Medem and Vladimir Senilov.[37] The first two were music critics and writers who had ties to *Mir iskusstva* and Diaghilev. Richard Taruskin describes Nurok as the 'spiritus rector' of the organization and a 'highly cultivated musical dilettante'.[38] Medem was a pianist, composer and professor at the St Petersburg Conservatory. Senilov was a composer. This introduction to an alternative world of musical sound and ideas would prove to be eye-opening and invaluable for the young Prokofiev.

This period marked the beginning of Prokofiev's introduction to contemporary audiences and he consumed the cultural influences, both musical and otherwise, of St Petersburg with greedy enthusiasm.[39] Doors continued to open for the young composer beyond his adopted hometown of St Petersburg. In Paris, Nurok, Nouvel and Vyacheslav Karatygin would continue to champion his music as the prime example of contemporary and cutting-edge music emerging from Russia; they were drawn to its vitality, vibrancy and athleticism.[40] Their support for the young pianist–composer – the introductions they secured for him – came at a critical point for the aspiring iconoclast and helped consolidate his image as an avant-garde composer. Prokofiev's first official public appearance under the auspices of the Evenings of Contemporary Music occurred in December 1908. He decided to play some of his own compositions since he knew that he caused most furore when playing these himself.[41] Prokofiev was always delighted when his music caused debate and he was careful to note which pieces attracted the most applause. He enjoyed the debate around his music because it generated and enhanced his reputation as a musical rebel, and later as a modernist. He relished 'provok[ing] much lively discussion' about his music because it gave him the opportunity to 'defend . . . it vigorously'.[42] It amused him to see that his music annoyed the more conservative authorities of the conservatory. Glazunov, the head of the St Petersburg Conservatory, who had been one of the thirteen-year-old Prokofiev's foremost champions, could not understand his (juvenile) symphony; he 'approved the first movement least, the second movement more so and the third still more. The first movement was too dissonant for him, particularly the second page of the exposition.'[43]

While he completed the last years of his conservatory training, the Evenings of Contemporary Music and its associated network remained a very supportive platform for him. Despite the opportunities that were now coming his way thanks to his connections, Prokofiev, perhaps surprisingly, and certainly ambiguously, continued to yearn for recognition within the conservatory. Most crucially, he still wanted acknowledgement and appreciation for his bigger compositional scores. To his mind, the conservatory had recognized him as a pianist but not yet as a composer. He considered himself to be both and wanted to be publicly perceived as a pianist–composer. His launch as a composer came early in 1910 – two years after his official debut as a pianist – when his op. 7 (*Two Poems*) was performed at an evening concert accompanied by an orchestra.[44] It was a huge source of pride for him: 'I was transmogrified into "the composer"; "the maestro", my stock in the Conservatoire rose rapidly, and I became a well-known figure within its walls, just as I had dreamed of before writing *The White Swan*. I was "a composer" who had written a "very beautiful" chorus.'[45]

Prokofiev set the *Two Poems* to the poetry of Konstantin Balmont, before he had even met the poet in person. (When the composer became friends with Balmont, he characterized him as a 'sunny soul'. The poet in turn dedicated poems to the composer, reciprocating by calling him a 'sun-voiced Scythian', referring to the harmonies and textures of the composer's writing.[46]) Balmont was the author of a collection of poems, 'Let us Be Like the Sun', published in 1903. Prokofiev's early pieces demonstrate a very different kind of orchestral timbre and colour palette in the composer's orchestral writing; the influence of both Scriabin and Strauss is clear. They were written at a time when the composer was experimenting with the creation of a new sound in his piano music. Although he was creating that very successfully in the enfant terrible phase of his piano writing, which included the *Sarcasms* and the *Toccata*, the music that he was writing for orchestra was significantly different. It is almost as though at this time Prokofiev experienced a musical split personality.

Later that month Prokofiev's Sinfonietta was included for performance in a subscription concert series – he excitedly noted these events as marking the start of his compositional career.[47] By November 1910 Prokofiev triumphantly wrote in his dairy that he was appearing 'in all my capacities simultaneously, as composer, conductor and pianist'.[48] These were inspiring and energetic years, and the composer identified Russia and later what would become the Soviet Union, in his own imagination at least, with the energy, inspiration and electricity of this period. Arguably, he continued to yearn for these perfect moments all his life. It is very possible that he craved a return to this spirit of unfettered creativity and inspiration when he made the crucial decision to return home.

2

Coming of Age

Of all the composers who have come out of Russia since the beginning
of the present century, Serge [*sic*] Prokofiev is the one who, more than
any other, typifies the ages in which we live.

Rollo H. Myers[1]

As he immersed himself in Symbolism and Scythianism, Prokofiev
commenced work on his ballet *Ala and Lolli*.[2] This was his first
commission from Diaghilev; he was tasked to work with the writer
and poet Sergei Gorodetsky, who was both a pagan symbolist as
well as a Scythian poet. In the post-revolutionary reimagination
of the term, Scythianism in Russia enabled a transition from
Symbolism to Futurism.[3] *Ala and Lolli* was eventually abandoned
and the music was reconfigured into the ever-popular *Scythian
Suite*. Nevertheless, Prokofiev remained intrigued by Scythianism.
He returned to Symbolist poetry for inspiration in his *Mimoletnosti*
(Visions Fugitives), op. 22, written for piano between 1915 and
1917. Polina Dimova argues that in *Ala and Lolli* Prokofiev follows
the Symbolist poet Konstantin Balmont's practice of 'conflating
colour, sound, and scent'.[4] In her view the chromatic twists and
turns 'paint the music'. From its first performance in 1916, *Scythian
Suite* was compared with Stravinsky's *Rite of Spring*; an irritated
Prokofiev often found himself responding to questions surrounding
the extent of Stravinsky's influence on his own work. While it is
natural that parallels were heard and made between the works of
the two composers, the underlying compositional methods are
very different and typical of each composer. Richard Taruskin has,

very concisely, identified two types of simplicity that characterize the writing. Stravinsky's *uproshchenie* was characterized by 'a breakthrough to the simplicity of a higher truth' while Prokofiev's *oproshchenie* was the 'crude simplicity of the barbarian'.[5]

This analysis of how simplicity in music operates in the compositions of these two composers further sets up a dichotomy between the very different stylistic approach to musical materials – with the implication that Prokofiev's music was somehow more uncouth and less developed than that of Stravinsky. It is a problematic analysis, as it glosses over Prokofiev's own approach to writing new material in the Scythian style as he had understood it through his deep, and at times personal, interactions with his connections in pre-revolutionary Petersburg. The composer creates a powerful and majestic sound with beautiful timbres from across the orchestra. With echoes of Stravinsky's primitivist approach in *Rite of Spring*, Prokofiev's *Scythian Suite* is unabashedly percussive, majestic, powerful and all-consuming; a work that was prophetic of the revolution that was about to take the world by storm.

Despite the abandonment of *Ala and Lolli*, Diaghilev did not lose faith in his 'second son', as he often called Prokofiev (his first son was, of course, Stravinsky). In 1915 he commissioned a new ballet, *Chout*, pairing Prokofiev with the choreographer Léonide Massine. Based on an Afanasyev folk tale, the story tells how seven buffoons are tricked by another buffoon into believing that the latter managed to kill his wife and then resurrect her with a magic whip. When the other fools kill their wives and it transpires that they are unable to bring them back to life, they seek revenge. Prokofiev's music is humorous and witty, full of fresh strokes of orchestration and impossibly real characterizations. The music evokes, quite literally at times, aspects of the scenes unfolding on stage.

The first version of the ballet did not convince Diaghilev and he suggested several changes and amendments, which Prokofiev took in his stride, acknowledging his lack of experience in writing for ballet (his previous large-scale work was the first version of his opera *The Gambler*). Crucially, in his focused determination to create his first impressive score for Diaghilev, he did not think through the practicalities of what would be required when composing for the genre (such as entr'actes for set changes, and so on). But Diaghilev even critiqued the music, arguing that it had an international sound, rather than a distinctively and exotic Russian one. Prokofiev reacted with surprise; perhaps naively, the young composer had assumed that Diaghilev had hired him to compose for his company because he was able to write music that was full of individuality and originality. But the impresario had little time for intellectual and aesthetic luxuries, insisting instead that his new protégé move to an instantly recognizable Russian sound as this would be far more marketable for the Ballets Russes enterprise. Prokofiev bristled at what he initially perceived as meddling, but soon trusted and accepted Diaghilev's judgement on this matter. After all, Prokofiev was an inexperienced ballet composer and he certainly had not grasped the underlying aspect of exoticism that made the Ballets Russes so popular; his concept of a specific Russian sound was far more subtle and organic. The First World War destroyed any possibilities of *Chout* being performed, even after he had made the changes requested.

After the First World War, Diaghilev's Ballets Russes occupied a liminal space within the heart of London's intellectual and artistic elite, moving from Covent Garden to the Coliseum, the Alhambra and the Empire Theatre. Having no fixed abode in London meant that the company was now perceived as entertainment, and as such had to compete with other forms of music-hall production in the British capital, which reduced the types of funding and patronage that Diaghilev had become used to relying on.[6] When presented in London, *Chout*, the grotesquely comic tale of the buffoon who outwits seven other buffoons, was out of sync with the spirit of the times. Through no fault of Prokofiev's, the audience *Chout* had been written for had outgrown the work and it was presented to the stage at a time when the British press was looking for home-grown ballets. The first performance took place in Paris in May 1921 by the Ballets Russes with choreography by the inexperienced Polish-born dancer Tadeusz Slavinsky and with Prokofiev at the podium; it received a lukewarm reception.

A significant influence on Prokofiev in the mid-1910s was his preoccupation with death. His indirect experience of death was made especially real and poignant by the loss of his close friend, and to some extent alter ego, Maximilian Schmidthof. A fellow pianist at the conservatory and one year younger than Prokofiev, they had been close friends since 1909. They got on well; Prokofiev considered him his intellectual equal as well as a kindred soul. They often spent their summer holidays together and Max participated in the joys and triumphs of Prokofiev's early career. The manner of his death was particularly theatrical: on 26 April 1913, the young composer received a note from Max, declaring, 'Dear Seryozha, I'm writing to tell you the latest news – I have shot myself. Don't get too upset and take it with indifference, for in truth that doesn't deserve anything more than that. Farewell. Max. The causes are unimportant.' This note stunned Prokofiev; he was haunted and troubled by Max's death far more than he was by that of his father. Prokofiev dedicated a number of pieces to his deceased friend, including Piano Concerto No. 2, which he had been completing at the time of the suicide. A very different person from Myaskovsky, the loss of Schmidthof seared Prokofoev with a profound, lasting sadness. He tried to remain in contact with Max's sister Ekaterina, corresponding frequently with her.

More emotional drama was to follow. The traumatic loss of his friend was followed soon after by Prokofiev's aborted engagement with Nina Meshcherskaya, a long-time close family friend with whom he spent many happy hours and was thoroughly in love with. Although Nina found Prokofiev somewhat awkward and eccentric initially, the adoration was reciprocated. Ultimately, however, this relationship was not approved by Nina's parents, who did not consider the couple a good match. The engagement did not come to anything. Their relationship is encapsulated in Prokofiev's setting of op. 14, *The Ugly Duckling*, written for voice and piano, to Nina's adaptation of Hans Christian Andersen's tale. Prokofiev's taste for compelling storytelling through motivic and rhythmic means demonstrates his maturity, even with a work that might seem as though it is for children. Lyrical lines work in tandem with

Lubov Tchernicheva and Serge Lifar in costume for *Le Pas d'Acier*, 1927.

the text-setting, and tight rhythms and structure hold the piece together.

At a point in his life impacted by both young love and tragic death, Prokofiev continued his immersion in some of the most influential ideas of Russia's so-called Silver Age (*c*. 1890–1924), perceiving in their symbols and imagery of death and transfiguration a very personal connection. He saw in the aesthetic of the Silver Age the possibility of a beauty that would enable

Sergei Prokofiev seated with members of the Reberg family, Sontsivka, *c.* 1909.

humanity to transcend the limits of reality and achieve a glorified higher purpose. During this period, Prokofiev created an album (the 'Wooden Book') as an autograph book for his friends to write short messages in. It was as if he wanted to get a fuller understanding of the motivations behind the different trends of the period from St Petersburg's key influencers. He challenged contributors to respond to the very specific question, 'What do you think about the Sun?' This somewhat baffling and naive experiment nonetheless demonstrates the composer's systematic and methodical way of thinking about prevailing concepts of the day. Through the responses of the various contributors, the 'Wooden Book' drew together elements of Scythianism, Futurism and Symbolism. Scholars have gone as far as describing the years 1913–16 as Prokofiev's period of 'sun worship', during which the composer explored and thought about the concept of Symbolism and the avant-garde. They were the years in which Prokofiev came of age, both personally and artistically.

Prokofiev, like many other composers, artists, poets and writers, immersed himself in the culture of the Russian Silver Age, whose 'outlook bred exaggerated hopes for Russia as a moral country'.[7]

Poetry and literature had always appealed to him; indeed he even wrote a number of short stories that demonstrate his gift for the pithy and ironic. To his mind, work born of a Silver Age aesthetic would allow for the realization of a spiritual and artistic goal. He also remained naively hopeful that culture in Russia would be allowed to flourish once the political questions were resolved and the country was under stable leadership. It was the hope of most, if not all, contemporary artists that they could be part of a constructive dialogue in the creation of a vibrant cultural life for a new Russia. But this hope too was utopian and unachievable. Tsarist retribution against terrorism and anti-monarchism was brutal and consistent, and, as the composer Nicolas Nabokov remembers in his own memoirs, 'the jails were full of scholars and intellectuals.'[8] The situation failed to change after the revolution. Although Lenin's initial and most important targets on ascending to power were ideas rather than people, the situation changed rapidly and chaos ensued in the decade that followed the Bolshevik seizure of power. Prokofiev may have remembered the hope and excitement that changes to the status quo were to bring, but when he finally returned to his homeland, he was to find out how terribly and irrevocably he had allowed himself to be misled.

Prokofiev's fascination with the musical possibilities of the human voice and its intersection with language and text-setting continued. In *Five Poems*, op. 27, he set texts by the darling of contemporary Russian poetry, Anna Akhmatova. Akhmatova wrote in a concise and restrained style characterized by emotional control. Prokofiev was drawn to her economy of expression and clear imagery. He premiered *Five Poems* with the soprano Zinaida Artyomova at a Concert of Modern Music in Moscow on 18 February 1917. These pieces were enormously well-received, with critics like Karatygin hailing their deeper lyricism and their instinctive poetry. Others were happily surprised to see the composer embrace a lyricism that they thought he did not possess. These works were composed swiftly, in only four days, after he had reworked *Ala and Lolli* into the *Scythian Suite*. No doubt they provided a welcome clarity and relief from the exertions and effort required to write his first ballet for Diaghilev. Prokofiev himself chose the poems included in this short cycle, selecting their order while focusing on the semantic as well as structural differences between them. According to Dimova, 'he reshuffle[d] earlier and later poems to depict the flowering, fading, and demise of love.'[9] It is worth remembering that at this time Prokofiev was undergoing his own personal emotional turmoil following his break-up with Nina. Perhaps Akhmatova's poetry enabled him to exorcise this relationship from his mind.

Prokofiev was equally enthralled by the poetry of Vladimir Mayakovsky, whom he had met after a recital given in Moscow in February 1917. The composer was mesmerized by the repetitive sounds of words in Mayakovsky's poetry, by the iteration of verbs to convey direction and energy to music and by the manipulation of pitches to play with combinations of vowels and consonants. Symbolist experiments continued for Prokofiev through and beyond his pre-revolutionary years. This fascination manifested in another key work of the period, the cantata *Seven, They Are Seven*, based on Balmont's poem 'Ancient Calls'. Prokofiev spent many months with Balmont himself critically dismembering the text to fully understand the layers of meaning and symbolism, which the poet had assimilated from multiple ancient sources. Prokofiev rose to the challenge and scored it for a large orchestra, chorus and tenor. It is a powerful demonstration of the composer's capacity for thinking about colour and structure on a large scale. His deep connection with the dramatic imagery and the musical opportunities inherent in it, in combination with his interest in mythology, is evident in the text chosen and in the ways that he chose to set it. The orchestration is majestic, bombastic even, capturing the feverish energy of these cataclysmic days as Prokofiev experienced them – not merely through his own eyes but through the artistic perspectives around him. It is uncompromising in its rhythmic drive and precise in its declamation, layering carefully crafted motifs (such as the choir's piercing interjections) and building slowly but surely into a devastating climax. To this day it surely captures the events of 1917 more compellingly than any other contemporary music.[10]

Prokofiev also admired the work of the Symbolist poet Andrey Bely (though when he was working on his opera *Fiery Angel* the composer was unaware that Bely was a figure in the *roman-à-clef* on which the work was based). Bely's long narrative and autobiographical poem 'First Encounter', frequently thought to be his best work, ponders Moscow at the turn of the century. This work had a profound effect on Prokofiev. Indeed, in September 1922, while continuing work on *Fiery Angel*, he reflected on his continued interest in Bely, noting that initially he found 'First Encounter' 'so obscure it was difficult to understand'. On picking the text up a month later, he 'discovered one sublimity after another'.[11] A day later he was completely spellbound by the work, endlessly quoting excerpts from it.

Prokofiev derived real pleasure and inspiration from exploring opera's links to both theatrical and literary traditions. He understood the importance of the visual image and maintaining a flow of movement on stage. He had clear ideas about the pacing and structuring of scenes within scenes, turning to concepts from the theatre world to explain his methods to journalists. Two of these concepts are theatrical rhythm and scenographic plasticity, both of which were important parameters in all of his operas, across all periods (even if they were more nuanced in his Soviet works). The composer sought a more fluid form of storytelling with pictures, where the onstage movement is not stilted but rather appears as real as possible. It is not difficult to see how Prokofiev would be attracted by the medium of film and be keen to write music for it. It would satisfy both his theatrical and his modernist aesthetics.

Although Prokofiev had written his first opera during his time at the conservatory, entitled *Maddalena*, it was never performed. It is a short opera with an overture and four scenes; only the overture and the four scenes were orchestrated. It seems that when Prokofiev wanted the St Petersburg Conservatory to stage this work, they considered it too complicated, and the composer was not at the time able to pursue its performance. But a passion like his was not to be deterred. Within three years he completed his first full-length opera based on Fyodor Dostoyevsky's novella *The Gambler*. At the time of its conception, Prokofiev was completely immersed in the culture of the period, attending evenings of literature and poetry reading; he was friendly with Vsevolod Meyerhold and other theatre directors, and was well aware of the developments and innovations in contemporary theatre. He had strong links to key figures from Diaghilev's *Mir iskusstva*, and the Ballets Russes founder continued to support his career for the next decade at least. His knowledge of the zeitgeist would no doubt have inspired him to think about the operatic form critically; he was keen to make his mark on the Russian scene. The pre-revolutionary days in St Petersburg were heady and fuelled by a sense of impending change and the composer thrived in this atmosphere of excitement, using it to inspire his own works.

It was the St Petersburg-born British conductor Albert Coates who urged Prokofiev to write *The Gambler*.[12] The two became friends around 1914; Coates, when he was conductor of the Mariinsky Theatre, was instrumental in pushing the composer to write his first mature opera, telling his Russian friend, 'Write your Gambler, we'll stage it!'[13] Perhaps unsurprisingly, Coates was also a composer (writing seven operas and some orchestral works), although he is not remembered as such. But this would explain his continued interest in and support for Prokofiev's operatic endeavours. In *The Gambler* Prokofiev experiments with many of the ideals that he cherished. He was faithful to the spoken word, avoiding arias and set ensembles. He expected each singer to have supporting acting skills that would enable them to bring their characters to life. Berating the current state of opera as an antiquated formulation of arias and recitatives accompanied by ineffectual acting, the young iconoclast took it upon himself to write what he hoped would become an opera for the contemporary world. He would later adopt a similar forward-thinking approach when he came to write *Semyon Kotko*, which he intended to be the first Soviet opera. In *The Gambler* he turned his attention to Russian sources and worked with the language to play with declamation and text-setting in ways that mirrored Mussorgsky's experiments in the genre. He adored Dostoyevsky's characters and considered the character of the grandmother, Babulenka, the most Russian of them all. Indeed, he made a pertinent point about this character in a contemporary diary entry: 'The aroma of Mother Russia must fill the stage from the moment she appears in her wheelchair.'[14]

The initial plan was for Meyerhold to direct this work. Prokofiev knew that Meyerhold would prioritize the rhythm of the action and also focus on linking gestures and movement with music, which to his mind was a much better way of aligning opera with the language of theatre. When Prokofiev started composing *The Gambler* he lavished great attention on the character of the Englishman, Mr Astley, whom he modelled on Coates. The British conductor was instrumental in smoothing over bottlenecks in negotiations, for example in the lithographing of the score of *The Gambler*. He organized the copying of the music, as well as the first and second run-throughs of the work, even bringing Meyerhold into rehearsals. In return, Prokofiev commented and listened to Coates's operatic drafts.

Crucially, while working on *The Gambler* Prokofiev was focused on the role of the Russian language itself. He was intent on creating a sound that drew self-consciously from his own musical heritage. He probed and played with the sonic essence of Cyrillic sounds, immersing and intertwining his melodic lines with precisely matched consonant sets. These sound combinations are paired exactingly with emphases in the bar, with orchestral phrasing, and precise instrumentation and rhythms. Prokofiev's initial influences may have come from the earlier experiments of Dargomyzhsky and Mussorgsky, but it was Prokofiev the Russian composer who successfully brought cohesion to these traditions. From the outset he characterized *The Gambler* as being a work that challenged opera's ordinary reliance on static settings and rhymed verse. He explained this in an interview at the time, which served as an artistic manifesto in many ways. He argued that opera was shackled by conventions from a previous age. In his view it was these crippling conventions that prevented opera from appealing to contemporary audiences. In his thinking, Prokofiev adopted a contemporary and critical approach: he argued that the genre should be more realistic, and singers should embody their characters, using techniques derived from the theatrical stage if necessary. He concluded that, because of the form's 'understanding of the stage, the flexibility, freedom, and declamatory expressiveness, opera should be the most vivid and powerful of the sonic arts'.[15]

Prokofiev interpreted the original text as literally as possible. This was a method he adopted in any work that required text-setting, partly because he loved the sonic possibilities of the Russian language, and saw its potential for distinctive shapes and combinations of sounds. To do this, he often took what Taruskin called 'melodic moulds', in other words, the melodic shapes that exist separately from the text yet are inspired by it. Prokofiev would then proceed to set the text very precisely to each melodic mould. In this way each character then had a unique inflexion, a particular, recognizable trait. When he came to orchestrate the work, he further pursued this method of declamation by using instrumentation as part of the characterization. Indeed, in his first three operas (*The Gambler*, *The Love for Three Oranges*, *Fiery Angel*) this was his normal approach. Working with text in such a painstaking and detailed manner enabled him to play with a combination of songs and rhythm, exploiting the ranges and quirks of the human voice. Often these are deployed to further delineate the characters themselves. In this way Prokofiev did not simply pursue the Russian traditions of declamation but brought them to an artistic culmination that others would hope to emulate.

Prokofiev's next opera, *The Love for Three Oranges*, was based on Meyerhold's adaptation of Carlo Gozzi's *fiabe teatrali* (fantastic plays or fairy tales). He made further tweaks to the Meyerhold adaptation to align it with his own concept of theatrical rhythm. He did not compose this work to contract but since Meyerhold was an influential theatre director (and at the time an official of the theatre division of the Commissariat of Education and Enlightenment), Prokofiev would have assumed that at some point the work would receive a premiere in the Russian theatres. After all, it had been Meyerhold himself who prompted him to consider making an opera out of the libretto. Prokofiev promised he would read Meyerhold's adaptation of the Gozzi fable and think about the proposal as he sailed to the United States in 1918 for his first tour. In his approach to setting the libretto to music, the composer focused on the text's inherent theatricality; his opera deliberately draws the audience's attention to the interdisciplinary approach he adopted when writing operas. *The Love for Three Oranges* draws on the fantastic tradition of Rimsky-Korsakov with very clearly Russian elements, such as the obvious use of the octatonic and sustained ostinatos. Prokofiev found the story's absurd elements enticing and was especially drawn to its theatricality – its interaction with the audience. Here again he remained true to his dramaturgical principles as they were explored in *The Gambler*, now layering the comedic element.

Prokofiev was not to be swayed from his operatic vision despite the difficulties he had with staging both *The Gambler* and *Oranges*. In his view, these obstacles were fleeting, and he would not allow them to shape or quash his ideas about this most beloved of genres. Speaking to an American journalist in 1920, he stated:

I believe in my theories of opera. I don't believe in arias and concert numbers being injected into the action of the music. It isn't natural. Why should an individual stop and say 'listen to my concert aria'[?] It's like putting lengthy and repeated speeches into a play. My opera has no arias. It progresses like the play. You see the cardinal virtue (or vice as you will) of my life has been my search for an original language of my own in music.[16]

These were uncompromising words given the taxing experience of the previous eighteen months. When this opera was produced in 1927 by the Mariinsky Theatre, he loved the production because it was full of 'inventive little touches', and he was satisfied 'that the production had been conceived with enthusiasm and talent'.[17] In *The Love for Three Oranges*, Prokofiev was able to really probe Meyerhold's philosophy of theatre. In essence Meyerhold aimed to challenge the way an audience understood and perceived reality, presenting paradoxes to disrupt the audience's coherent understanding of the world around it. In this sense, like Prokofiev, Meyerhold sought to

Sergei Prokofiev (centre) with the cast of *The Love for Three Oranges* at the Leningrad (St Petersburg) Opera and Ballet Theatre, 1926.

enable curious and critical audience members to take a deep dive into the theatrical experience.

However, once again Prokofiev's ideas for the performance of this second opera were sabotaged by events beyond his control. He was working on this opera even before he had left Russia, writing about it to the esteemed music critic and publisher Vladimir Derzhanovsky in early 1917. The composer took the work with him to the United States, continuing to work on it while touring. He managed to secure a commission from the Chicago Opera via its director, Cleofonte Campanini, in 1919. When the director died in December that year, contractual complications ensued and the opera was not premiered until 30 December 1921, with the composer as conductor.

This experience of attempting to get *Oranges* onto the stage taught Prokofiev a great deal about self-belief, the worth of one's art and, crucially, entrepreneurship. There were many delays and arguments over contracts during this period; it would appear that the administration of the Chicago Opera was not willing to pay what Prokofiev was initially promised and what he considered a suitable amount. Negotiations around the finances and other contractual niceties delayed the performance. The Scottish-American soprano Mary Garden (a successful singer and a household name in America who achieved fame for being the first Mélisande in Debussy's *Pelléas et Mélisande*, which premiered in 1902) wanted the opera staged properly, believing in its orchestral innovation, effervescent colours and quirky scenario. She intervened to help Prokofiev in her capacity as company director of the Chicago Opera Association. Garden was ready to acquiesce to the composer's wish for more rehearsals and full artistic control. By September 1922, nearly a year after the debut of *The Love for Three Oranges*, Prokofiev had signed a contract with a German agency guaranteeing that the opera would be performed across six opera houses in Europe by summer 1923. The experience scarred Prokofiev and instilled in him a determination to ensure that his work was adequately paid for and that he was not taken advantage of. He suffered much anxiety during the traumatic negotiations, which, although he had advice from friends, he had to pursue and complete on his own. He eventually obtained the contract that he wanted but much time had passed since the work's completion and *Oranges*, like the ballet *Chout*, is an example of a commissioned and completed work whose first performance ended up taking years to materialize.

Opera was the love of Prokofiev's life and his passion for it lasted, quite literally, until the day he died. It was success in opera that he pursued most tenaciously and persistently, often throwing caution to the wind, and usually ignoring well-meaning advice from friends and peers. This obsession is manifest in the relentless pursuit of performances for works that he had written, like *The Gambler*, *The Love for Three Oranges* and *Fiery Angel*, to somewhat tenuous or even non-existent commissions. The composer wrote all his librettos often without collaborators (until he found a partner in his second wife on his return to the Soviet Union). He selected plots because they appealed to him, often simply because he found the characters appealing, convincing or humorous, or because there was something compelling in the landscape of the text that he could easily convert into a soundscape, as was the case with *Fiery Angel*.

3

Scythian on Tour: Early Travels and Beyond

Your arrival is a profound joy for us; your music, like the scorching sun, spontaneously burns the soul and one wants to weep in delight.
Adolph Bolm[1]

Even though he was deeply inspired by his St Petersburg aesthetic set and intellectual connections, Prokofiev did not take his eye off the international scene. He knew that if he was to achieve success, like his predecessor Scriabin for instance, he would need to curate and sustain an international reputation.

As early as June 1913, Prokofiev set off for his first visit to London; he missed the premiere of Stravinsky's *Rite of Spring* by a few days. He travelled with a largely Russian contingent on whom he relied for help with his inadequate English-language skills. During this first trip to Europe, Prokofiev, with his usual eye for the strange and unfamiliar, saw an opportunity to look at Russia through the lens of an outsider, even though these trips were made in the company of other Russians. But even as he conducted this theoretical exercise, his heart and mind were unerringly Russian; even in these very early days of travelling, Prokofiev reflected on the pleasure of hearing the Russian language being spoken – an unexpected comment perhaps, but a telling one.[2] A year later he undertook his second trip to Britain, and on 9 June 1914 he docked at Newcastle and took a train to London. In his diaries he confessed that he 'had come to London knowing that Russian music was all the rage now, and of course I was hoping to make some connections in that field'.[3] Prokofiev was in London for a month. Not one for doing anything by halves, he embraced the city's lifestyle, enjoying coffee with a roll and butter, honey and jam for breakfast, after which he would get on the 'omnibus' and head to the offices of Breitkopf, where he had been given space to compose.[4] At the time he was working on a revision of the Sinfonietta, a four-movement piece for orchestra that he had written in 1909, during his early period. He played bridge, walked in Hyde Park and attended the Russian theatre, as well as the occasional music hall and, not least, a boxing match. On Sundays, he went out of town, 'like all properly brought-up residents of London', delighting in trips to Windsor and Kew Gardens.[5] He enjoyed shopping until he ran out of money. His primary intention, although he was atypically coy about it, was to meet Diaghilev in person and obtain a commission for new work. He clearly expected that the impresario would open up international opportunities for him, as he had seemingly done for Stravinsky. His first meeting with Diaghilev, the 'brilliant entrepreneur', whom he found to be a 'supremely elegant figure in top hat and tails', happened in London.[6] After this meeting, Prokofiev related the details warmly in a letter to his close friend Myaskovsky; his excitement at being given backstage access to all performances was palpable.[7] A year later, Prokofiev explained to Myaskovsky that the most progressive trend, 'embraced by both Stravinsky and Diaghilev, is now this: down with pathos, down with grandiosity, down with internationalism. They are turning me into the most Russian composer there ever was.'[8] Perhaps at this early stage, and at a time when he was still seeking new ways of making a name for himself, Prokofiev considered his Russian identity to be malleable, and at the service of art.

Prokofiev decided to depart from Russia and start his international touring and concertizing at a politically difficult time; his reminiscences from one of his domestic tours tell the poignant story of how challenging it was to earn a living as an artist at a time of conflict. By mid-1917, following disappointments on numerous artistic fronts (including the cancellation of several concerts), and with St Petersburg constantly under threat of attack from the Germans, Prokofiev decided to spend the winter with his mother

in the southwestern city of Kislovodsk.[9] Sensing his artistic career
was on hold before it even took off, he decided that he should go
to the United States. As he put it, 'Here was wretchedness; there
life brimming over. Here, slaughter and barbaric rhetoric; there,
cultivated life. Here, shabby concerts in Kislovodsk; there, New
York, Chicago! No time for hesitation.'[10] Leaving the country was
difficult but not impossible; Prokofiev was never one to be daunted
by challenges. However, to leave Russia one had to first make
the fraught trip to Petrograd. Prokofiev needed to traverse areas
controlled by Bolsheviks and Cossacks, but his determination knew
no bounds. Always proactive, he began to explore the possibility of
a Serbian passport to make his journey to the United States a more
realistic prospect.

That the composer was determined to leave Russia at this time
is clear: pragmatic even at a young age, his motives for departure
were largely financial. He argued that the only reason success in the
United States was important was the 'external, specifically financial,
perspective. Internally it would be of minimal value, since the
musical perceptions of the Americans are not sufficiently refined

Sergei Prokofiev at the piano, Nikopol, 1910.

to cause me to pay much attention to them.'[11] Despite his scornful comments about American audiences, he would soon realize that Anglo-American reception would provide a more analytical and balanced view of his music, while French reception would prove to be both fickle and supercilious.

Nonetheless, given the Russian rouble's weakness, the strength and reliability of the u.s. dollar was beguiling. Prokofiev gradually formulated a plan to go to New York via a tour of Japan. Weighing his prospects of concerts alongside possible collaborators like the Ukrainian singer Nina Koshetz, Prokofiev decided to spend as little time in Japan as possible, in favour of a longer time in America:

> Since in the present state of communication with Russia nothing can be relied upon, America is at present the horse I have to put my shirt on, particularly so as there is more point in performing to audiences who understand something (although actually I do not have all that much faith in the understanding of the American public) than to Asians and semi-Europeans.[12]

In the midst of chaos, Prokofiev continued composing. Soon after his arrival in New York in September 1918, he was commissioned by the Zimro Ensemble to create a piece for a sextet. The *Overture on Hebrew Themes*, op. 34, is scored for the unusual combination of clarinet, string quartet and piano.[13] There is an urgency in the composing of this work because it was, as he puts it, one way out of 'beggary', which he hated so much. When Diaghilev sent him an advance towards his ballet *Chout* in 1916, Prokofiev's glee was palpable: 'Never have I had in my hand at any one time more than 500 roubles, and now suddenly I have three times that amount. Fantastic.'[14] A couple of years later, still not self-sufficient by any means, the ups and downs continued: he went from 'having no money at all' and sustaining himself occasionally on 'some biscuits I happened to have', to experiencing the 'marvellous feeling' of having $100 in his pocket.[15]

For Prokofiev, the early 1920s was characterized by an almost constant need for funds. In the post-war years, this would be a predicament familiar to many artists; Prokofiev was no exception. Although he continued to contemplate and even write new works, a great deal of his time was spent performing (because it was a good way to earn money), ensuring the works he had written in the previous decade were staged and that his royalties were paid. Prokofiev calculated that a u.s. debut in 1919 would require $2,000 (around $35,000 today) for general publicity purposes.[16] The first task on his to-do list was to procure a manager who could obtain this kind of cash flow. He agreed to hire Rachmaninov's manager as his first manager in New York for a fee of 10 per cent of his earnings. Prokofiev apparently had another manager, Jessica Colbert from San Francisco, California, who seems to have been sufficiently in control of his business affairs. She sent him cheques in a relatively timely manner and they sustained a cordial relationship. He did nonetheless chide her for not attending his concert, stating that 'women never keep their appointments.'[17] He reminded her to send him a cheque for $400 for another engagement he had undertaken. Looking through the archival sources and materials that are now available to us, it is clear to see that he was juggling many spinning plates, an approach to life and work that would soon become unsustainable. His later long-standing American manager, Fitzhugh Haensel, would take 15 per cent, eventually increasing that to 20 per cent. Adding to his financial struggles during this post-revolutionary period, debts to the Russian consulate for obtaining visas accumulated – money needed to bring his mother, who was trapped in the Caucasus, to the United States. Sending funds to his mother, who he feared was a destitute refugee trapped between Bolshevik fighting, was a constant preoccupation during this time. Her ticket alone would cost him $400 (equivalent to around $7,000 today).[18] Russian friends in New York stepped in to assist but his recitals were also running at a loss. He wrote ruefully, 'The concert yielded a loss of $200 (box office takings $350, expenses $500). Not much of an improvement over last time. But many people suppose in their naivety that it has made me a rich man.'[19] Concerts booked across three weeks in early 1920 (when the inflation rate was 15.91 per cent) amounted to $1,200 (around $18,000 today) which Prokofiev considered would be enough to live on for three months.

Unlike other Russian émigrés who managed to smuggle some of their family wealth out of Bolshevik Russia, Prokofiev had no family funds to rely on. His mother's pension provided for their immediate needs and all other funds came from his own compositions and performing activities. Prokofiev had produced an incredible amount of significant works by 1920. In the previous twelve years he had built an impressive oeuvre across all genres and sought to obtain performances for these in the 1920s; he also programmed and played his own works whenever the opportunity arose. He had every reason to expect that this body of compositions would begin to yield some income.[20] Orchestral works included the ambitious *Seven, They Are Seven*, op. 30 (1917–18, revd 1933), as well as the *Humoresque Scherzo*, op. 12bis (1915) for four bassoons, and the *Overture on Hebrew Themes*, op. 34 (1919) for clarinet, string quartet and piano. Few of these orchestral works were regularly performed, except for those programmed by the ever-supportive Albert Coates and Serge Koussevitzky, who remained an important figure in Prokofiev's career. Koussevitzky supported Prokofiev in his early days and introduced his work to American audiences; he continued to ensure the composer's music was heard in the USA even after Prokofiev had returned to the USSR.[21] It was Koussevitzky who presented Prokofiev to Paris on 29 April 1921 at the Salle Gaveau, where the orchestra played the *Scythian Suite*. Later, advances for commissions received from Koussevitzky enabled Prokofiev to survive on composition rather than expending any more precious time and energy concertizing.

Prokofiev demonstrated himself to be a quick learner when it came to dealing with agents and publishers.[22] He was determined to survive and succeed and no opportunity was left untapped; he drew on his friendship with Coates to broker his entry into Britain and America, following in the footsteps of other Russians like Rachmaninov and Scriabin to conquer new audiences. Coates found opportunities for Prokofiev to play in New York and in London, but he also mentored him in the ways of British society, counselling

him on the right people to cultivate friendships with. For example,
Coates introduced Prokofiev to Lady Cunard, an American society
hostess and heiress based in London, and instructed him to ensure
that he enlisted her support as a cultural patron.[23] She agreed to see
if she could help him stage *The Gambler* at Covent Garden. Prokofiev
took this society mingling in his stride and did his best to follow
instructions, although that did not stop him from mocking the
artistic patrons that Coates tried to connect him with. Meanwhile
Coates regularly prodded the Russian for new works, particularly
looking for shorter works that he could include in his concert
programmes. Prokofiev, for his part, found that 'performing with
him was unalloyed pleasure'.[24] When the composer arrived in
England in May 1920, the first person he called was Coates, who
took him to Covent Garden the very next day, because he wanted to

do everything in his power to support Prokofiev and to ensure he was connected with the right people who could advance his work. Prokofiev reciprocated those sentiments.

During these early years, Prokofiev relied heavily on networks of benefactors who were impressed by his music and sympathetic to his story – an informal type of patronage that was the only way an exile could survive and thrive, particularly in contemporary America. In New York he was befriended by Alexey Stahl, who was formerly a public prosecutor of the provisional government. Stahl's wife was the Greek-Brazilian soprano Vera Janacopoulos. The Stahls opened his eyes to the possibility of working and performing in South America. They remained close friends with the composer and met up regularly when he was in New York.

Just as Prokofiev made his first appearance at Carnegie Hall, he also performed his Piano Concerto No. 1 – which he later described as 'somewhat weaker musically than the other two but effective enough for provincial performances' – with the Chicago Symphony Orchestra under the conductor Frederick Stock.[25] These engagements were organized by Cyrus McCormick, another important supporter of Prokofiev, who enabled many of his early appearances in Chicago. As his benefactor of sorts, he also introduced him to the director of the Chicago Opera, Campanini. These local contacts were a source of continued solace for an artist like Prokofiev who was out of his element and by all accounts always an outlier in social situations.

In the United States, Prokofiev found another, welcome, source of income: the creation of piano rolls with the Duo-Art company. Some contractual and financial bargaining ensues here too, with a typical Prokofievan sense of humour:

When the director suggested I play him four pieces for a fee of $50 each, I replied with great good humour that since my concept of a fee differed so radically from theirs, I would naturally not play for that money. However, if they agreed to pay me properly, I would be pleased to play for nothing. They did not immediately understand my little joke, and for a moment thought they were going to walk off with a good profit scot-free. The American soul is dollar-shaped; here even honour comes wrapped in a dollar bill.[26]

Eventually they settled on $250 a roll (around $4,000 in today's currency).

By the early 1920s, at the grand age of 29, Prokofiev aimed to secure a living from royalties and performances of his works; his intent was to sustain himself and those who depended on him while he moved on to new compositions. But this was not as straightforward as he had hoped. Financial struggles continued to put a strain on him for quite a few years, certainly until he was able to afford a business manager-cum-secretary who would handle these administrative processes for him. Initially, while attempting to stay one step ahead of poverty, Prokofiev had no choice but to do it all himself. Later, Prokofiev's main artistic manager was Haensel & Jones in the United States; in Europe he continued to liaise personally with the heads of publishing and recording houses (such as Duo-Art) as well as with other impresarios. These included Vladimir Zederbaum, a former doctor, who had worked as a secretary for Serge Koussevitzky in America. Having had a falling out with Koussevitzky's wife Natalia, Zederbaum was now managing the European branch of Koussevitzky's publishing business, Russian Musical Editions.

4

Transitional Years

To roam the roads of lands remote,
To travel is to live.
Hans Christian Andersen[1]

While Prokofiev was forging a name for himself on the international stage in the 1920s, his personal life was flourishing too. A critical moment for the composer occurred in 1918 while performing in New York. This was his meeting with a young singer called Carolina (Lina) Codina, the woman who would become his first wife. Six years younger than Prokofiev, she had an intriguing and complex genealogy: her father was Spanish, and through her mother she had French, Polish and Russian heritage. An intelligent, cultured and sophisticated woman, she spoke those languages fluently and moved through ambassadorial and expatriate circles with ease and fluency. She was, in short, the polar opposite of Prokofiev, who immediately fell for her charms and courted her persistently. They married in a non-religious and simple ceremony in Ettal, Bavaria, on 29 September 1923. She was pregnant at the time and Mariya Grigoryevna's health (Mariya was living with her son at this time) was also in a precarious position. Prokofiev now found himself having to care for his mother as well as for his wife and a new baby. Despite these challenges his time in Ettal was a happy one, and Prokofiev wrote to Natalia Koussevitzky of his interest in the outdoors and in raising chickens successfully: 'Let me tell you some news: I have purchased an electric incubator for 60 "individuals," which has been in operation for 14 days now . . .

Sergei Prokofiev and his first wife, Lina, 1923.

We are terribly proud of our successful rooster, and at a general gathering granted him eternal life plus a pound of oats.'[2]

Sadly, his mother died on 13 December 1924. He marks the day with poignant but surgical precision in his diary: 'At 12:15 in the morning Mama died in my arms.'[3] No further entries were made that year while he took the time to grieve and readjust. Even as his personal and home life stabilized, and while his wife was on very friendly terms with the international community of artists around her, Prokofiev struggled with the very principle of an émigré community. He uncompromisingly and often unceremoniously observed that the émigrés in exile in Paris were limiting themselves in many ways, especially in their quest to integrate with local developments in music. He continued to remain aloof from them, commenting on several occasions in his autobiography that moving to Paris did not mean becoming a Parisian. He was scornful of émigrés and their plan to rebuild Russia anew, disdainfully noting in his diaries: 'And these émigrés see themselves as the future builders of the Russia of the future! God forbid.'[4] In his memoirs, the composer Nicolas Nabokov would often explain to people who asked him about the Russian Revolution that he, his mother and most of their family left Russia in 1919 and had no intention of ever returning. This was the general émigré approach to the revolution. Those who had managed to escape, most of them intellectuals, artists and scientists, had no plans to go back. When Nabokov returned to the Soviet Union much later, he saw nothing to make him regret his decision to go into exile and he continued to refer to himself as a 'rootless cosmopolitan'.[5]

On his return to Europe in 1920, Prokofiev was aware of, and certainly crossed paths with, many of the recent émigrés escaping the Russian Revolution. Many families were dispossessed and travelled to London, Paris, Berlin and Rome, creating a new Russian diaspora. These artists relied exclusively on their talents to survive because, as Vladimir Nabokov famously declared, 'even genius does not save one in Russia; in exile, one is saved by genius alone.'[6] In Paris, during his travels to London and beyond to the USA, Prokofiev made friends and acquired admirers who were in

Sergei Prokofiev, 1918–20.

positions to offer substantial assistance that was both monetary and social.

Among his friends was Pyotr Petrovich Suvchinsky (later known as Pierre Souvtchinsky), a writer, philosopher, entrepreneur and patron. Suvchinsky was close to a number of Russian composers, including Prokofiev, Myaskovsky and, most famously, Stravinsky, for whom he ghost-wrote *La poétique musicale*. He left Russia in 1922 and settled in Paris, where he continued to be involved in contemporary music. Suvchinsky was a powerful intellectual of the Russian émigré community and he became a lead figure in the Eurasianist movement in Parisian circles. The underlying notion behind this movement was that Russians owed more to their Asian heritage than they did to Western civilization and, as a Eurasianist entity, Russia had a unique identity. As the scholar Marlène Laruelle observes, 'Eurasianism uses a highly flexible terminology that hides a variety of currents, which are distinct both ideologically and sociologically.'[7] The origins of this intellectual movement took root in exile and, ultimately, it was a philosophy of exile that could only flourish within a community of people undergoing a process of self-estrangement from their homeland. During this period, while

Eurasianism focused on theorizing the exilic experience, Prokofiev did not espouse the concept of being estranged from his homeland, voluntarily or otherwise. He was also unpersuaded by theoretical thought that was, at least to his mind, largely inactive and not in service to his art. He preferred having full agency over his identity: he maintained strong enough connections with the people building, as he saw it, music education and culture in this new Russia as to make estrangement and exile unrealistic concepts for him.

Suvchinsky did not give up on changing his compatriot's mind. He spent a great deal of time discussing the movement with Prokofiev in an effort to broaden his interest in and deepen his intellectual understanding of exilic life in France, and what this life and future might hold for those who had severed ties with Imperial Russia. He also shared his views on Bolshevism freely with Prokofiev and Lina. Simply put, within the contemporary Eurasianist mode of thinking, the Bolshevik Revolution was almost an inevitable means to balance and purge the increased Westernization of Russian society. Eurasianism swiftly caught the imagination of those exiled from Russia. Berlin, rather than Paris, became an outpost for the Russian intelligentsia because it maintained connections to the homeland. The city had everything an émigré community could need in its time of transience: Russian newspapers, theatres, places of worship, literary clubs, publishing houses and groceries, as well as Russian foreign-exchange speculators. Nonetheless, this pervasive Russian culture did not penetrate the lives of the Berliners in any meaningful or sustained manner. The situation for the émigrés in Paris was very different and it was to this environment that Prokofiev was exposed. What he saw of émigré life in Paris did not persuade him that this was a suitable or sustainable way of life for him or his family. He was not wealthy enough to reside in hotels in the style of a 'rootless cosmopolitan', as both Stravinsky and Nabokov were accustomed to. Most significantly, he wanted to compose and hear his work performed; for him, this was non-negotiable and related directly to his own self-estimation as an artist. The series of mistimed appearances and productions of his work in France frustrated and exhausted him beyond measure. Moving within the gaudy and provocative intellectualism of interwar Paris did not appeal to him – for him this was simply living a fashionable half-life. He continued to think about and actively consider a return to Russia; he dreamed of returning to an admiring audience who respected his work, and to a full roster of performances that would include staging his operas, which continued to languish in his drawer.

From the moment he bid his fond – but not, to his mind at least, permanent – farewell to pre-revolutionary Petersburg, Prokofiev occupied an ambiguous and unsettled position that made him neither émigré nor Soviet. For two decades, he moved between émigré circles in France and America (notably Paris, New York, Boston and Chicago), while also meeting and maintaining contact with Soviet citizens who visited Europe on official business. As far as possible, Prokofiev retained an open mind about the development of the young Soviet Union, referring to himself as apolitical on several occasions. In truth, he was sufficiently exasperated with his position in the West to, at the very least, be willing to listen to ambassadors who gave the artistic exiles the latest news on the cultural development of the Soviet Union. In one discussion about contemporary politics, where all his friends spoke against the Bolsheviks, Prokofiev declared that he 'heard them with interest, while not trying to take sides myself'.[8] He was painstaking in his separation of the political from the artistic. It soon became evident to the émigré communities in Berlin and Paris that a power struggle within the upper echelons of the young Communist Party was taking place after Lenin's death. One of the immediate and more practical consequences, certainly for those who were not yet sure about the regime and the direction it was taking, was the difficulty of travelling overseas: it became more complicated for most Russian citizens unless they were part of official delegations or possessed a Nansen passport. These passports, in use between 1922 and 1938 and normally issued for one year, enabled stateless refugees to travel and were a response to the influx of refugees entering the West from Russia after the revolution. In this way artists, musicians, writers and painters were able to take their art and practice out of Russia and seek ways of integrating with new communities.[9]

Sergei Prokofiev, 1918.

Possibly because of his itinerant lifestyle or perhaps because of his character, Prokofiev did not have many friends – but those he had were fiercely loyal to him. The composer sustained correspondence with individuals from his conservatory years, such as Vera Alpers, Eleanora Damskaya, Nikolai Myaskovsky, Boris Asafyev and others, who kept him appraised of the changing cultural conditions in Russia. From 1923 onwards Prokofiev strengthened his correspondence with important figures in the newly minted Soviet Union who now occupied important positions within the new regime. It was to them that he turned to understand how music was developing back home. After the revolution his old friend Vladimir Derzhanovsky, who ran the Moscow equivalent of Evenings of Modern Music in the pre-revolutionary years and also founded the periodical *Music* in 1910, had joined the music division of Narkompros, which was the ministry responsible for art, science and education. He was tasked with running a music section that imported foreign books and exported Soviet publications. He was also, for a short while at least, in a position to determine contemporary concert programming. Derzhanovsky arranged concerts that featured Prokofiev's Piano Concerto No. 3 and his Violin Concerto No. 1, among other works. Even while he was away from Russia, Prokofiev's music continued to be programmed, performed and heard by the upcoming generation of composers and musicians. Other connections with the Russian musical world continued through the Association for Contemporary Music, which was a concert organization, similar in spirit to the French ones, established precisely to perform the best of new music by Western and Russian composers.[10] The composer certainly had no reason to feel alienated from the artistic and cultural developments in the Soviet Union as they were being represented to him from numerous sources.

Part of the composer's connection to his Russian identity, such as he envisaged it, relied on his ability to maintain meaningful connections with his old friends and the musical culture he remembered even while he was physically separate from them. Staying connecting was so important to Prokofiev that even in the chaos of his arrival in New York in 1918, he wrote to Myaskovsky within a fortnight. Sadly, this was followed by a five-year hiatus in their correspondence. As Nelly Kravetz has observed, there were several reasons for this, including a mundane possibility: the composer simply lost Myaskovsky's address. But even as Prokofiev persevered in locating Myaskovsky through his friends and close networks, his friend experienced several changes in his personal life. In 1918 his father died while on business and he had to move from St Petersburg to Moscow, living in different locations; for a long time Myaskovsky did not have his own residence. The correspondence between Prokofiev and Myaskovsky did not restart until 4 January 1923 but it then lasted until the end of Myaskovsky's life in 1950.[11] Through their frequent correspondence, Prokofiev felt that he knew what was going on in the new Soviet state. After all, by 1921 Myaskovsky held the position of professor of the Moscow Conservatory, while Asafyev continued to compose and later became a prominent Soviet musicologist. Prokofiev's music was also consistently played by the conductorless Persimfans orchestra and the composer himself performed with the orchestra in 1927, on his first return tour to the Soviet Union.[12] These connections would no doubt have made Prokofiev feel sufficiently informed on musical life in post-revolutionary Russia, despite his physical absence from his homeland.

As early as 1924 Myaskovsky had written to Prokofiev to suggest a staged performance of his early opera *Maddalena*. Although this did not materialize, other Prokofiev works were performed. This is not to give the mistaken impression that the composer was adored by all following his departure from Russia. His exacting standards, uncompromising attitude and strong opinions did not immediately endear him to people. Some argued that his music reflected the artistic ideals of an outdated period; others like Grigory Krein dismissed Prokofiev as 'an anti-musical fellow'.[13] But the ones who mattered and whose voices were respected in the Soviet Union at this time, including Myaskovsky, Asafyev and Derzhanovsky, regarded Prokofiev as the most significant composer of the period and of their generation. They continued in their unwavering admiration and support of his work.

Prokofiev was eager to get on with writing a new work and he waited for a commission from the dancer and ballet impresario Ida Rubinstein, hoping that it would provide some much-needed income: 'If only I had myself to worry about,' he fretted, 'the financial situation would not have been causing me much concern, but now that I have people dependent on me at both the dawn and the sunset of their lives, this question weighs heavily on me.'[14] On the occasion of the birth of their first son, Sviatoslav, Lina Prokofiev received 3,000 francs (around €450 today) from a rich American friend, Mrs Garvin, to cover the expenses of the birth and confinement. While Lina was embarrassed to take the money, Prokofiev was relieved that the funds came at such a timely moment for their household. During these quieter days, where performing and earning an income were an utmost priority, he still made time for reading and reflection alongside his regular piano practice, thinking about how far his musical style had departed from Scriabin and how much closer it had become to Stravinsky with his 'fabulous technical mastery' (as he describes it pensively in his diary).[15] Continually searching for the best possible artistic trajectory, he debated with himself: 'What is the true path for the artist – to penetrate ever deeper into his own mastery or ever wider into the expanse of the cosmos? Scriabin or Stravinsky? Both, united in one!'[16] On other occasions he worried about conservatism or academicism in his music, a quality that he abhorred in Glazunov's and hated in that of the 'fossilized' Medtner.

Stravinsky was equally fascinated by his younger compatriot. Nicolas Nabokov remembers Stravinsky interrogating him about Prokofiev, on whom he kept a close, although not always supportive, eye. When Nabokov explained that he had become close friends with Prokofiev and had even shown him drafts of his music, Stravinsky was displeased. According to Nabokov, Stravinsky said that although he did like Seryozha Prokofiev, as he preferred to call him, his music was 'so uneven . . . Not only uneven, there is something *primaire* about it . . . And at times uncouth . . . its spirit is alien to me.' Stravinsky ended this admonition with the advice to the aspiring composer not to let himself be influenced by Prokofiev because it would not be healthy for his own music, arguing, somewhat paradoxically, that Prokofiev's music was 'also lyrical, but never gentle'.[17] Stravinsky enjoyed finding out what Prokofiev was up to without asking him, relying instead on the gossip of their mutual friends. While at lunch in June 1924 with Suvchinsky and the librettist and choreographer Boris Kochno, Stravinsky gossiped about Prokofiev's insistence on being a modernist, a term understood in their circles to signify the most novel approaches and fashions in contemporary music. The older composer preferred to consistently make out that his younger compatriot lagged behind the latest trends; this was partly true, but nonetheless the younger composer was not finished with innovation and certainly had not yet put his iconoclast days behind him.

A galvanizing moment for the young composer occurred in May 1924, when he heard the Swiss composer Arthur Honegger's *Pacific 231*. Such was its impact on Prokofiev that he continued to ponder it for days afterwards, declaring it 'a good lesson to learn, and I must really buckle down to instrumentation and inventiveness'.[18] Prokofiev was nothing if not deliberate in his approach to composition, carefully determining the development of his style. Honegger's masterwork had come at a time when Prokofiev was surrounded by the chatter of modernism, a term that, as always, he understood in his own way. In truth, he abhorred labels and categories of all kinds, shunning their determinism and shackling of his creative freedoms. While working on his ballet *Prodigal Son*, Prokofiev reflected on this and articulated it with great precision:

The term 'modern' music used to be attached to the search for new harmonies, then moved to the search for beauty in all kinds of insincere contrivances and complexities. More perceptive composers soon tired of this and went back to seeking simplicity – not, however, the old simplicity, but a new one. Diaghilev of course was with this new wave.[19]

Whenever Prokofiev interacted with any established movement, modernism being the most obvious example, he always refracted it through his own personal lens – unless he owned it, he would not use it. It is at this point that the composer began to contemplate his arguably most daring composition yet, Symphony No. 2. It is also hardly surprising that Prokofiev, with his love for all things mechanical and modern, would be enthralled by *Pacific 231*. Many devices would have resonated with him at first hearing, including the use of brass in the instrumentation and the carefully calculated and deliberately paced crescendo sustaining the work to its climatic moment. Symphony No. 2 was commissioned by Serge Koussevitzky and was separated from Prokofiev's Symphony No. 1, known popularly as the Classical Symphony, by seven years. While Symphony No. 1 was written as a personal challenge to see whether he could compose away from the piano, Symphony No. 2 was, for Prokofiev, almost more of a moral challenge than a musical one. In this symphony, the composer explored the extremes of modernity in music, partly as he understood them, but also experimenting in response to what he heard in Paris at the time.

On completion of the second symphony he complained, 'two hundred pages and nine months' work. When I started on it, I thought it would take three! I feel like a gymnast who has got through a gruelling test.'[20] This work proved to be a critical failure at its first performance. Prokofiev experienced a rare but severe moment of self-doubt, pensively considering that 'this was probably the only time it occurred to me that I was fated to be second rate.'[21] The fear of being thought of as an inferior composer haunted him throughout his years in Paris, because, as we have seen, he felt artistically, aesthetically and even personally misplaced. In the end, he concluded, the symphony 'was too densely woven in texture, too heavily laden with contrapuntal lines changing to figuration to be successful, and although one critic did comment on the septuple counterpoint, my friends preserved an embarrassed silence'.[22] Once it was completed, Prokofiev, with a muted sense of relief, turned to new projects.[23]

Prokofiev was a misfit in Paris and was constantly looking over his shoulder, whether for professional or personal reasons. While he harboured no doubts about writing modernist music, it is not a label that he was at ease with, preferring to keep his distance from 'schools' of modernism and remain focused on his own individuality, which he always felt was the heart and soul of his creative practice.[24] In adopting this stance he remained detached from the French context and contemptuous of the aesthetics and music of Les Six.[25] 'But my God, what music!' he commented after an evening of music by Georges Auric and Francis Poulenc.

> It consists entirely of barrel-organ trifles, facile and vulgar doodles in which it is hard to detect any composition at all. And yet, unlike the work of some provincial Kapellmeister there is an element of contrivance behind it: it pays lip-service to the peculiar, snobbish style currently fashionable in Paris at the moment, a style that needless to say will tomorrow wither away.[26]

Behind the contempt, however, Prokofiev was frustrated at his own perceived stagnation: 'composers like Stravinsky, Honegger, Auric, [Vladimir] Dukelsky always present themselves in Paris with new works, whereas I seem to be everlastingly condemned to stale goods like the *Scythian Suite*.'[27] He was concerned about the lack of rehearsal time available to French orchestras, especially when Koussevitzky informed him that he would be able to have as many as ten sessions in the United States. On such occasions, Prokofiev no doubt reminded himself, and perhaps took comfort from the fact, that he would much rather be taken seriously by the Anglo-American critics and audiences than the supercilious French.

In 1925 Diaghilev had commissioned another ballet from Prokofiev, despite the relatively unsuccessful reception of *Chout*. This time, and in a nod to contemporary politics, the impresario asked him to create what he called a 'Bolshevik' ballet, but one to be written in Prokofiev's own style. The original scenario was titled *Ursignol*, a play on the French name for the Soviet Union: l'URSS (Union des Républiques Socialistes Soviétiques). It was titled *Le Pas d'Acier* in French and translated to *Steel Step* for Anglo-American audiences. Scenic designs and artistic concept belonged to Georgii Yakulov, an

Armenian set designer and painter who had lived and worked in Moscow and was thus assumed to have the most accurate insider's view of life in the new Soviet Union, more than either Diaghilev or Prokofiev. The composer collaborated with Yakulov to create a scenario that was approved by Diaghilev. The impresario eventually found the émigré choreographer Léonide Massine to work with Prokofiev on this project. As Lesley-Anne Sayers demonstrates, Massine made a number of changes to the original scenario and designs.[28] Whether or not Prokofiev was aware of the ironies of writing a composition celebrating workers' lives in the Soviet Union (of which he had, as yet, no direct experience) while being part of a company (the Ballets Russes) that was subsidized by white émigrés and those still loyal to Tsarist Russia, is immaterial. It was essentially an imaginative creation that enabled Prokofiev to work on another project for Diaghilev that would be produced on a French stage before going on tour. He did have sufficient insight into the situation to seek advice from Suvchinsky about this 'delicate' project, nonetheless. Prokofiev considered Suvchinsky not only knowledgeable about theatre and music, but 'well-informed' about everything unfolding in Russia in 1925. He characterized the project as

> so acutely contentious that there would be no chance of creating a neutral work; it would have to be either a White ballet or a Red ballet . . . it would be impossible to find a neutral standpoint acceptable to both sides, since the Russia of today is dominated by precisely the struggle of the Red faction against the White, from which it follows that any attempt to represent an objective approach would not accurately reflect the moment.[29]

Perhaps then, the contradiction inherent in this commission was not lost on him, even if it was not a topic he spoke about publicly and in the press at this time. Nonetheless, this was an essential career move and the pragmatic composer was not about to start criticizing Diaghilev's decisions, having now been with the company for a decade. The music is compelling, full of Prokofiev's signature orchestral moments and thrumming with rhythmic energy. But the work was not taken seriously – possibly because of the awkwardness in having émigrés create a work about a life they knew nothing about. Instead, critics and audiences focused on its excessive modernity, its constructivist sets and its choreography of mass scenes. Reviews described it as 'the last word in ugly modernity. The choreography by Mr Massine is infernally clever in its gymnastic gestures . . . [Eugene] Goossens conducted the bizarre music brilliantly, and the large audience was deliriously enthusiastic.'[30]

Amid the continued ups and downs of his life in Paris, Prokofiev pondered with warmth and some comfort the news coming to him from the ussr via his old friend Myaskovsky, where he was told that his music continued to be popular with Moscow audiences. Asafyev would say the same about the reception of his work in St Petersburg. In 1925 Piano Concerto No. 3 was played in Moscow; its success was reported back to Prokofiev by Derzhanovsky and the composer

Jean Cocteau and Sergei Diaghilev on the opening night of *Le Train Bleu*, 1924.

was delighted.[31] In the meantime he continued to write to Asafyev about the possibility of staging *Oranges* at the Mariinsky Theatre.[32] Nonetheless, Prokofiev was not yet ready to return home with anything less than a successful international career. He stayed on in Paris, keeping up with local trends and attending premieres of the works of important contemporary French composers, in particular Les Six. But most of these spectacles and trends did not convince: 'it is all of a piece with these "new" directions, the point of which escapes me.'[33] Time and again Prokofiev argued that in his view Maurice Ravel was the greatest French composer. He also did not get on particularly well with literary Paris, especially the likes of Jean Cocteau; possibly because Cocteau was connected to Stravinsky, but more likely because Prokofiev did not easily relate to that kind of French literary modernism. He thought Diaghilev's latest offering, *Le Train Bleu*, was 'a deliberate essay at vulgar material orchestrated in a vulgar style' and continued to feel baffled by the impresario's contemporary productions.[34] It is in such sentiments that we may find the clues to Prokofiev's periodic introversion and reflection.

Prokofiev despised being 'fashionable' just for the sake of it, arguing that innovation and 'contrivance' that withers away the next day was far less valuable than ingenuity and authentic innovation. He understood opinions shifted constantly, and pondered this:

Time was when people used to complain about anything new, but now everyone is so accustomed to endless novelty that the composer is censured if his latest compositions fail . . . History, however, teaches us that composers, once their style has evolved, maintain it for the rest of their lives, and this was considered an admirable trait betokening an individual personality, a unique voice. Such were Haydn, Schumann, Chopin.[35]

This quality, he felt, should be respected regardless of whether that composer was fashionable or not, considering in 1926 that a 'wholesale rejection' of Scriabin would be wrong. He held himself to those same strict ideals. He resented the need to make a simplified version of the March from *The Love for Three Oranges*, finding that the 'process of denuding for the sake of simplicity is highly disagreeable'.[36] On his return to his homeland, Prokofiev would not easily change his mind, although he would speak of this complex concept far less directly. By late 1928 Prokofiev made a deliberate decision to develop and foreground certain concepts in his music over others – he needed to 'compose in a quite different style' and would do so 'as soon as I had extricated myself from the revisions of *Fiery Angel* and *The Gambler*'.[37]

Prokofiev was introduced to Valery Bryusov's novel *The Fiery Angel* (1908) by a New York émigré acquaintance of his, Boris Samoilenko, in November 1919. The composer was immediately drawn to its medieval German atmosphere; in his diary, he regarded the novel to be 'very good'.[38] He also approached it with some sense of nostalgia because, as he recounts, it had been quite a while since he had been in possession of any Russian books. Within a couple of weeks of his first read-through of the novel, the composer was considering using it as a plot for a new opera. He recognized that the opera would need to 'express high drama and terror but avoid bringing any devils or apparitions on to the stage, otherwise it risks toppling over and collapsing into pure theatrical sham . . . The scenario demands a great deal of very careful thinking.'[39] The composer thought long and cautiously before deciding to embark on his new project.[40]

However, Prokofiev did eventually take it on, and continued to work – albeit intermittently – on *Fiery Angel* for ten years, during which time the structural conception of the work changed, even if the language and musical ideas behind it did not. In *Fiery Angel* we see a composer whose love for the dramatic and theatrical sweeps all else (including sensible narrative plots) aside. In this powerful and immensely imaginative work, Prokofiev places all his energy in Renata, the half-witch, half-Madonna femme fatale protagonist of the opera, who belonged to the same genre of female lead roles as Strauss's Salomé and Elektra. Beyond all else, he sought to explore her thoughts, her ideas, her aspirations – using his artistic language to probe deep into her psyche and play with a number of possibilities, including her madness. Prokofiev gave himself free rein when it came to exploring this element of Bryusov's narrative, and Renata's part demonstrates the hallmarks of the composer's writing for the female voice. At once beguiling, seductive and maddening, Renata destroys everything in her path that does not take her to a reunion with her beloved Fiery Angel. To this day, the role is taken on by very few experienced voices and charismatic stage actors.

During these early years of fatherhood, Prokofiev continued to focus on making a successful career for himself with the aim of providing adequately for his family. His diaries from this period are touching in this regard as he returns, time and again, to his desire to own a small house or farm outside Paris with a large garden and outbuildings. And yet, these years were strenuous too. His health was not particularly good; he suffered frequently from headaches that appeared to be connected with neuralgia, he had frequent troubles with his teeth and his eyesight was getting poorer. His relationship with Lina was sometimes strained and he tried as much as he could to curb his focus on work and give her the attention she desired. For her part, Lina thought Prokofiev was a 'slave' to his work to the detriment of his family. Lina adopted Christian Science as her religion, having been introduced to it by British acquaintances. She started practising after the birth of her first son, Sviatoslav, and was under the care of the Christian Science practitioner Caroline Getty in June 1924. Her training included positive thinking and the prescription and teaching of meditation techniques that would allow her to concentrate on the body as immortal mind. Getty introduced Lina to other practitioners as well as to two local Christian Science congregations in Paris. Later, other practitioners entered the Prokofievs' lives and household – and they would have a decisive influence. After resisting the religion for some time, Sergei realized that Lina had discovered a philosophy towards life that was based on logic and reason.

Perhaps to his surprise, Prokofiev found great benefit in espousing Christian Science. He was particularly hopeful of its potential to offer self-healing and control over his own health but achieved very little success in improving his vision and controlling his chronic headaches, the pain of which he tried to alleviate with

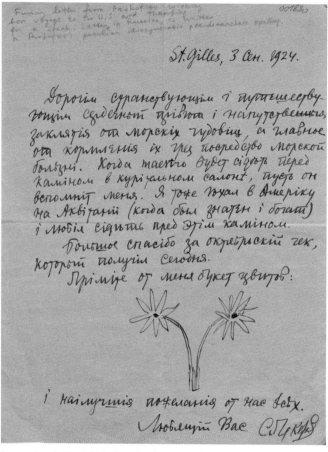

Letter written by Sergei Prokofiev in his idiosyncratic form of shorthand, 1924.

meditation. He realized that the religion was able to assist him in regulating his temper and he was intent on reducing his arguments with his wife. Although his efforts at self-healing remained largely unattained, the couple continued their devotion to Christian Science together. In 1924 they attended lectures; Prokofiev preferred to attend these in place of regular church services. The information he took from these lectures had a lasting impact and informed several of his own professional and personal choices. In particular, he found great consolation in the idea that if he as an artist was a reflection of the divine, then so was his art.

The only disconnect with his spiritual life at this point was his continuing work on the opera *Fiery Angel*, the story of which brings into conflict the natural and supernatural world – Christian Science did not allow for or recognize supernatural happenings. In fact, he wrote to his assistant Georgi Gorchakov, a young composer and musician who was devoted to Prokofiev and who was also a follower of Christian Science, that due to his commitment to Christian Science he had completely lost interest in the subject, with its fits alternating between hysteria and possession. Lina, however, encouraged him to focus on its musical innovation and to complete the work rather than get rid of it. The result was Symphony No. 3.

The equilibrium of the Prokofievs' marital relationship now appeared to rely on their joint practice of Christian Science. Conflicts were reasoned, their arguments lessened and their 'quarrels', as the composer called them, were over quickly. Lina suffered from her own anxieties, and Prokofiev accommodated her on any tours they undertook together, sometimes taking unprofitable engagements simply to allow her an opportunity to further her own career. The composer trod carefully around Lina and was solicitous of her well-being at most times.[41]

The 1925–6 season marked Prokofiev's first return to the United States and was an extremely busy one. He and Lina sailed to New York for a fourteen-concert tour of America. This tour was organized and enabled by Serge and Natalia Koussevitzky, who were working and adjusting to American business models and musical life. Indeed, seven of these appearances were with Koussevitzky and the Boston Symphony. Prokofiev's American manager, Fitzhugh Haensel, also managed to set up five recitals for him for which he received enough to avoid poverty, as he dryly noted. On this occasion American audiences were perhaps more cognizant of Prokofiev's maturity and received him far more warmly than on previous occasions. It no doubt helped that Prokofiev was sponsored by Koussevitzky, with whom American audiences were enamoured. Despite receiving an enthusiastic welcome and being lavishly entertained, the composer still felt that American audiences veered towards the conventional and conservative, fearing innovation and that which was new. He wrote quite bluntly of the American musical scene, declaring, 'you all ride in automobiles, and yet you lag behind in music. I would prefer you rode in horse-drawn carriages but were more up-to-date in music.'[42] During this period Prokofiev also had the opportunity to meet influential conductors such as Arturo Toscanini, Otto Klemperer and the pianist and conductor Alexander Siloti, who had all also relocated to America after successfully fleeing Russia in the wake of the Bolshevik revolution.

In 1926 Prokofiev engaged his first secretary, Viktor Labunsky, who was soon replaced by the composer Georgy Gorchakov. Gorchakov brought stability and organization to Prokofiev's financial and business matters, particularly as, at this time, the composer started to see royalties come in more regularly for works that were being performed both in Europe and in America, largely thanks to the championing of his friend Koussevitzky. At long last, Prokofiev began to experience some measure of financial stability, although he was no closer to owning a house in France.

Having spent a great deal of time and energy in the early 1920s conquering the West, Prokofiev's desire to prove himself tapered somewhat by the late 1920s. Soviet biographers have characterized these years, especially the late 1920s, as ones of 'travel', during which the prodigal son was sowing his wild oats musically, so to speak. These years of exile, as previous biographers have referred to them, deserve our attention for reasons that are personal rather than political. As we have already seen, Prokofiev worked hard in the years after the First World War to carve a sustainable and performance-based career for himself. These early years of struggle were also marked by ill-health, including hospitalization with scarlet fever and diphtheria.

Prokofiev's network of Russian connections in Europe helped in this regard but money and funding for the arts were scarce after the war, and the composer continued to hustle in order to achieve

Left to right: the Swiss conductor Ernest Ansermet, Sergei Diaghilev, Igor Stravinsky and Sergei Prokofiev, 1921.

the fees he felt he deserved for his performances as a pianist and conductor. He persisted in seeking conducting opportunities for himself and by the late 1920s he was in high demand as a performing pianist and could therefore command an appropriate fee. Securing performances of his works, especially his new ones, however, was an entirely different proposition. His operas, written at inauspicious times for companies that might seek to take them on, continued to be sidelined. The U.S. experience of *The Love for Three Oranges* had badly bruised Prokofiev's ego and he was somewhat more pliant when the Théâtre La Monnaie in Brussels approached him about a first performance of *The Gambler.* This led to his revising the work to create a second version, the one that is in the repertoire of opera houses today.[43] But even this experience was far from smooth. As for his non-commissioned but much-beloved *Fiery Angel*, Prokofiev, though not for want of trying, would never see the opera staged in his lifetime.

By 1926 Prokofiev was earning a reasonable wage that allowed him to maintain a comfortable life, although no more than that. Artistically as well as personally, he felt a renewed need to explore new challenges and to follow many of his refined musical thoughts and ideas to their logical conclusion. Balancing a life on the road with a young family and sustaining an entrepreneurial approach to his career was far from easy. One could argue that Prokofiev's modernist style achieved its apex in the piano pieces and in Piano Concertos Nos 2 and 3, works that remain unrivalled in the piano repertoire to this day. For him, the artistic challenges had been met but he was still only approaching the midway point in his career; there was no doubt in his mind that the time had come to set himself new artistic challenges.

Until the late 1920s, Prokofiev was still working incredibly hard even on a mundane and practical level, although his assistants were now more involved in securing performances for works that had been written and sat on the shelf for far too long. Such works included *The Gambler* and *Fiery Angel*, Symphony No. 2 (composed in 1924–5) and Symphony No. 3, which was extracted from *Fiery Angel*. Although Prokofiev's Diaghilev ballets were popular, they were not enough to sustain a living, not least because those ballets were also of their time. It is clear that Prokofiev was constantly trying to find ways in which he could get his music performed. In his habitual and thrifty approach to his compositional process, he also crafted Symphony No. 4 from the ballet *Prodigal Son*. He also created a suite of music from *The Gambler* and another from *Le Pas d'Acier*.

There are a number of reasons that works he composed during the 1920s in different genres remained largely unperformed, some of which were practical. In an economically strained interwar Europe, mounting productions of large stage works like operas and, after the death of Diaghilev, ballets, was difficult. Furthermore, in interwar Paris, the focus was more on what made French music French, with preference, naturally, often being given to home-grown composers. By mid-1925 Prokofiev had noticed that Diaghilev had made the decision to align with what the Russian composer called 'the French Group – Poulenc, Auric, [Darius] Milhaud. Stravinsky backed Poulenc and disparaged me – why is incomprehensible, but so it was.'[44] Prokofiev was not one to change viewpoints swiftly or erratically, so Stravinsky's frequent shifts would have taken him by surprise. He continued to hold steadfast to his own artistic originality, refusing to compromise it in any way. His contempt for borrowing, quotation and even allusion knew no bounds. In a candid letter to his friend and confessor, Myaskovsky, on 4 August 1925, he declared that 'Stravinsky has written a horrifying piano sonata. It's some kind of Bach covered with smallpox.' Not to be outdone, during a discussion of Prokofiev's Second Symphony with the young composer Vladimir Dukelsky, Stravinsky observed that Prokofiev had failed 'to break free of Mussorgskian pathos and Korsakovian Russianness'.[45] To an ear as sophisticated as Stravinsky's, Prokofiev's type of reconfigured Russian sound was clearly audible. Therefore, it is hardly surprising that Prokofiev found himself caught in-between: an exotic Russian, but ultimately an exile (since he would not commit to self-identifying as an émigré), and in some ways an impostor at a time when French nationalist music was on the agenda for music societies, promoters and the critical press. The composer's American agents repeatedly urged Prokofiev to include compositions by non-Russians and other composers in his programme. Inevitably, since he was hardly interested in performing for its own sake, he always gave these works his own personal interpretation, which was often at odds with what American audiences expected. In a letter to Vladimir Zederbaum, Koussevitzky's friend, agent and secretary at the time, he explained:

> Playing classical repertoire would be the greatest poison for me, and I request to be relieved of it. I am running out of time, and I will play mediocrely. As for expanding my Russian repertoire, it's not that simple. Adding modern pieces wouldn't make much sense, and among the Russian piano literature of this period, there is practically nothing to find . . . It may seem strange that I offer a repertoire that is not mainstream but rather a peculiar selection of pieces that may not receive the same success as other, more popular combinations . . . it should not be forgotten that every performer excels in what is close to their heart. If I am forced to play something that I don't feel called to, I will perform it as a second-rate pianist, cursing my fate.[46]

As early as 1925, under the auspices of Anatoli Lunacharsky, the People's Commissar for Enlightenment, the regime began to reach out to key artistic figures, not just composers. The plan was to formally invite such international personalities to visit the newly formed Soviet Union, possibly on a more regular basis. While Stravinsky immediately rejected such an offer (principally because he had no sympathies for the regime whatsoever), Prokofiev did not. He, unlike Stravinsky, was intrigued to find out more about the cultural and musical communities being formed in this new country. In 1926, Prokofiev crossed paths once again with the writer Maxim Gorky (they had met in St Petersburg before the revolution in 1917), who was living in Capri for health reasons. At this time Gorky was not in great health and had been told he had only ten years to live. His unique reputation and position as a writer had saved him from the fate of several other Soviet artists and his freedom was unprecedented; he was a proletarian writer living abroad, returning frequently to the Soviet Union to make rousing and powerful speeches in front of various organs of the state. He returned to Moscow permanently in 1931. It is hard to imagine that Prokofiev and Gorky would not have discussed the new Soviet state and its cultural direction during their meetings. The composer would also no doubt have been heartened (and misled) by the fact that Gorky was a Soviet artist living abroad. He may have thought, naively, that this was something he could emulate; however, the Soviet Union put a stop to the practice in the mid-1930s.

Prokofiev found the lure of his homeland hard to resist. The Bolsheviks had been making soft attempts to reach out to a number of Russians in exile. Even though Prokofiev continued to remain aloof from the émigré community, he spoke with Suvchinsky often on the topic of emigration. He stayed in contact with his cousins the Rayevskys throughout the regime change.[47] In 1926, he pondered his continuing relationship with his Russia: 'If I am so close to my native soil, it is no wonder I feel so alienated from those who have severed their links with it.'[48] It was in this frame of mind that he turned his attention to the Soviet Union and accepted to return on a tour, a momentous event to him on a personal level. He knew, however, that he was breaking new ground in returning to visit the newly built USSR and decided to chronicle his three months there in 1927 in a special diary.[49] After some bureaucratic and scheduling complications, it took place in the spring of 1927.

When he was contemplating the details of his tour to the USSR, some of his closest friends, such as Boris Bashkirov, were appalled that Prokofiev was considering going to Russia, but his retort tells us a great deal about his frame of mind: 'If you had the opportunity to go to Russia, to see again the places of your native land, to see your friends, just to stroll round Moscow and St Petersburg, and then freely to come back here again, would you really not want to go?'[50] He was beguiled by reports of his popularity in Moscow. When Boleslav Yavorsky (head of the music division of Lunacharsky's Narkompos – that is, the Ministry of Culture) came to Paris, Prokofiev was happy to treat him to a lobster lunch while the latter reminded him that he was as popular as Tchaikovsky. The composer also was supportive of the newness and vulnerability of Soviet culture. When Yavorsky asked him more directly whether he would consider touring Russia, Prokofiev replied that he was 'not particularly exercised about the financial conditions of the offer, as [he] considered it inappropriate at the present time to try to squeeze too much out of starving Russia'.[51] He wanted to travel back to Russia to meet Russian musicians and exchange ideas while showing them what he was doing; he envisaged a meeting of cultural and artistic minds. Nonetheless, he was not nescient and his chief concern was to have a cast-iron guarantee that he would have free passage in and out of the country. He was aware that some travellers with no particular political affiliation had experienced some difficulties when trying to leave the country, but in his lengthy discussions with Yavorsky, Prokofiev was repeatedly assured that there would be no obstructions to him travelling abroad.

Prokofiev wove in and out of émigré communities, but he never depended on them, considered himself part of them or shared their sensibilities. At times he could be quite supercilious about them, but his independence demonstrates that he never saw himself as an exile, rather as an international cosmopolitan whose artistic practice took him far beyond the borders of what was formerly Imperial Russia and now the Soviet Union. He was wary about getting too involved with the émigré community and he wanted to avoid being categorized as one of them, since he sensed that this would not be well received with his artistic and cultural peers (as he still thought of them) in the young Soviet Union. Indeed, in his diary he wrote, 'It is extraordinary how fashionable it has become among the émigré community to tell indecent stories; this is something that people coming from Russia never do.'[52] He knew, however, that when the time came for him to make the choice, it would be either Russia or permanent emigration; faced with this choice, he concluded, 'it is clear that it must be Russia.'

It is common in Prokofiev scholarship for the composer to be characterized as either naive about politics and the unfolding of events in the newly formed USSR, or as egotistic enough to think that he was untouchable. The truth, as always, is far more complex and nuanced than that. As we have already seen, the composer never lost touch with his connections in Moscow and St Petersburg. He continued his correspondence with Myaskovsky, which was his most sincere, consistent and revealing relationship in letters. He also corresponded with his long-time friends from the conservatory, Asafyev, Derzhanovsky, Alpers, Damskaya and others. He ensured that he was in touch with artists who had gone back to the USSR and then returned to Paris throughout the 1920s. These included Alexander Borovsky, a former student of Esipova and a personal friend. Prokofiev was a valuable, if complex, commodity for the Soviet state. His worth and artistic currency changed according to the broader, although at times subtle, cultural directions of the time. He was chased almost from the moment he left, as though the Bolsheviks immediately regretted authorizing his departure.

On this first visit in the spring of 1927, Prokofiev delighted in reconnecting with the St Petersburg that he remembered, reflecting on the beautiful architecture and atmosphere, now tinged with echoes of the recent revolutionary upheaval:

> How beautiful the Elizavetinsky Palace is! We admired it for
> a long time. But one of the adjacent streets has been renamed
> Byeloborody Street in honour of the communist who authorised
> the shooting of the Tsar's family. This is very tactless: if for some
> reason it was considered necessary to shoot children as well as
> adults, surely you don't have to celebrate it publicly.[53]

Both Lina and her husband thought the rumours circulated by the émigré community to be vastly exaggerated, but, equally, they were not wide-eyed. In his diary, Prokofiev noted that he felt 'at all times solidly conscious of the fact that the Bolsheviks are adept at showing off in order to impress foreigners'. He compared notes with Lina 'in whispers. We do not believe the rumours current in émigré circles to the effect that the beds have microphones fixed under them; but we do notice a locked door between our room and the next through which someone could easily eavesdrop if they wanted.'[54]

Serge Lifar and Felia Doubrovska in *The Prodigal Son,* performed by Diaghilev's Ballets Russes, 1929.

Prokofiev's trip to the Soviet Union in 1927 was a success, certainly in terms of his reconnection with the places, memories and friends of his youth.[55] The trip was a catalyst for the composer's re-evaluation of his current artistic identity, which was always on his mind. In that respect, this first trip to his homeland reawakened his deep connections with the country of his birth, and from this point on it was never far from his thoughts. He returned in 1929 for another tour. One can surmise that during these visits Prokofiev was looking eagerly around at this much-changed world, trying to situate himself and visualize what a permanent return to the Soviet Union might look like for him. He would have been particularly observant of the opportunities that might come his way while being mindful of what that might mean to his artistic freedom. At no point would the composer ever have agreed to sacrifice his freedom; nevertheless, it was also important for him that he would be able to earn a living from his music.

After his first tour, not much changed for Prokofiev. He continued juggling a profession as an international performer with composition, piano practice, managing his career and, of course, supporting a family and his wife's career as much as he could. Although Prokofiev could not have known this, he participated in what was to be the Ballets Russes's last Paris season. Diaghilev, its impresario, died in 1929 and the Ballets Russes disintegrated. Its legacy was reconfigured in other ways but for Prokofiev the loss of Diaghilev, an early mentor who really understood his musical ethos and identity, was shattering. The composer had only just internalized and personalized the genre of ballet in a way that he was content with. But this was not to last. The *Prodigal Son*, or *Le Fils prodigue*, op. 46, was based on the parable of the prodigal son, to a libretto by Boris Kochno, and was choreographed by George Balanchine. In a letter to Warren Klein, Prokofiev spoke of 'composing music for a theatrical piece the subject of which is taken from the bible – the parable of the Prodigal Son'. He continued, 'It is seldom that I have worked with such pleasure as I did on this piece.'[56]

The premiere of this ballet took place in May 1929 at the Théâtre Sarah Bernhardt, Paris, with Prokofiev conducting. Despite him

Always on the move, the Ballets Russes dancers stand with Sergei Diaghilev in 1929, the year the impresario died.

disagreeing with Kochno's dramatization of the parable and being unhappy with Balanchine's choreography, the work was a success. The title role was created by the Ukrainian dancer and choreographer Serge Lifar, one of the greatest male ballet dancers of the twentieth century. In this ballet we see a mature Prokofiev not only thinking through his experience of ballet as a genre, but embracing the development of a sound that would continue to be exclusively his. There is no mistaking Prokofiev's musical fingerprint in the harmonic turns, long lyrical lines and sublime orchestration. He embraced the lyrical bent in his music and exploited it in the most unpredictable and touching ways. Of special note is *Prodigal Son*'s reunion scene, with deliciously swirling and intertwining melodic lines on woodwinds, supported by an ever-increasing intense and harmonically tight accompaniment.

To his dismay, the epithet of 'ugliness' raised its unpleasant head once more in a contemporary review of the ballet:

M. Serge Prokofieff in his music has supported M. Georges [*sic*] Balanchine's choreography in queerness and ugliness. Everything about M. Prokofieff is queer. He showed us in his 'Chout' and his 'Le Pas d'Acier' that he hankers after gruesome subjects . . . here and there are signs that the composer has something to say.[57]

Today, these seem ill-considered remarks about a ballet that showcases the beauty and inimitable lyricism of Prokofiev's writing. One might well wonder whether the press in 1929 had a vested political interest in criticizing the music so harshly. From a compositional perspective, when working on *Prodigal Son*, Prokofiev decided to make a distinct change in his style, 'eschewing sophisticated elaborations'.[58] He wrote swiftly and smoothly, finding the process essentially trouble-free. But such was the contemporary perception of the composer's music – lacking in melody, possibly formless and definitely raucous. Gruesome, hardly; grotesque, perhaps, at times, but certainly not in this work. But in a diametrically opposed review we are assured that the

music made no great impression at a first hearing. It is surprisingly dull in the sense that the scoring has not that bright edge which has characterized most of his music. All he seems to have done is to provide good rhythms for dancing and then to have stood modestly aside.[59]

When Diaghilev died in 1929, Prokofiev lost a supportive – if critical – ear and a devoted promoter of his music. The founder of the Ballets Russes was well known for succeeding at staging works, as well as for finding sponsorship and entrepreneurial backing. Without Diaghilev's practical support for his creative projects, Prokofiev was unable to sustain a steady income stream from these ballet works. Nor would he be able to rely on the impresario's irreplaceable knack of understanding context and predicting aesthetic trends. It is thus unsurprising that after this rupture Prokofiev was drawn to a place of safety; a place where commissions with secure performances would be made available to him. He was at a time in his life where he had achieved much of what he wanted by way of performing and establishing himself as a modernist. Now he wanted to focus on exploring the full extent of his artistic identity. His main concern now – whether he articulated it to the press or not – was on his legacy. This period of the late 1920s, therefore, coincides with Prokofiev's renewed analysis and self-evaluation of his own artistic language, which in some areas of scholarship has been characterized as 'the new simplicity' style. This concept has been problematic and divisive in the study of the composer because it was appropriated by politically motivated commentators to imply that his previous music was somehow too complicated and modern to be sustainable. This, however, is not quite what Prokofiev meant when he spoke about simplicity in his writing. The composer had always been a lyricist, even though in the early works other aspects of his music, including its rhythmic and motoric drive, its ferocious energy and of course his own incredible performance of it, suggested that his music belonged more to the Futurists and the avant-garde (in its broadest sense of challenging traditions in favour of innovation) than to any other aesthetic. But as Prokofiev matured from this post-conservatory phase, he looked inwards for inspiration and growth.

Prokofiev's last ballet from his years in Paris, *Sur le Borysthène* (On the Dnieper), op. 51, is a ballet in two scenes with a prelude and epilogue. The work was instigated by the Ballet de l'Opéra National de Paris. The premiere took place in 1932 but it only had a handful of performances before it was relegated to a quiet corner of the composer's oeuvre. The ballet in many ways is the epitome of his lyrical gift; it is characterized by poignant and expansive lyricism, clear orchestral textures and no trace of compromise in his harmonic writing. It is structured as a series of twelve numbers, intended to intersect with the storyline. The loose-fitting storyline may initially have promised freedom to both composer and choreography, but Prokofiev was soon to find out that sustaining a convincing narrative was a far more complicated endeavour.

This ballet previews a clarity in his writing (especially the fifth number, 'The Betrothal') in which the instrumentation is dwelt on lavishly, a feature that has often been portrayed as emergent only during his Soviet years. As was his wont, Prokofiev crafted an orchestral suite from the work, op. 51bis. But after Diaghilev's death the composer was, as he put it in his diaries, 'less inclined towards the ballet',[60] and he was not to revisit writing in the genre until a few years later, with the Soviet commission of *Romeo and Juliet.*

Prokofiev's notebooks and sketches from this period demonstrate that his enduring instinct for lyricism is the foundation upon which his idiom was built. It is clear from a detailed examination of these notebooks, which provide an incredible insight into his compositional process, that Prokofiev was interested first and foremost in the lyricism and the melodic essence of a piece. Once these melodies had taken shape in his mind, assuming characters and taking on the mantle of orchestration, he would think about broader forms and structures for the work. Within this context, his concept of new simplicity was merely a way of revisiting the essence of what made him individual and original. His melodies remain unparalleled. They provide inspiration for contemporary composers and film composers: his melodies seem ubiquitous, and they appeal to listeners on many levels, musicians or otherwise. Prokofiev's lyricism can be heard in mainstream media: in adverts for Chanel and Coca-Cola, and as the opening theme of *The Apprentice*, to cite just the most famous and easily accessible examples. The composer Dmitri Kabalevsky remembers in this regard that,

> Prokofiev was a bitter enemy of all that was dull, insipid, sentimental and pretty in art. He demanded originality, inspiration and bold ideas. He always remained true to himself whatever genre he worked in, yet he had a keen sense of the specific requirements of the given genre and audience.[61]

The 1929 return visit to the Soviet Union gave Prokofiev the opportunity to delve deeper into some of the subtleties that he was not able to address or explore on previous visits. He noticed that Meyerhold was more agitated and more specific with his instructions to Prokofiev about how best to behave. The composer himself was not immune to these challenges and ambiguities, often wondering which topics of conversation were appropriate and which were not. He was also beguiled by a younger generation of theatre artists and producers who showed great interest in producing his *Oranges* and *The Gambler*. Prokofiev had no reason to distrust these approaches and plans as they were often accompanied by firm fees and contract offers, which in itself was very different to what the composer was accustomed to in Europe and America.

Despite his experiences, Prokofiev adhered to the thought that his music was 'international' and should be performed and understood by audiences as such. He had no wish to play to the tune of Parisian spectators and theatre goers. Public opinion of its nature is hardly ever consistent and he knew this well. Prokofiev was not prepared to sacrifice individuality and integrity in musical identity and style at the altar of public opinion. His core artistic beliefs, present throughout his entire career, were immutable and often landed him in difficult situations, both with his peers and later with various people in the USSR. Although he did benefit from the support and friendship of networks of Russian exiles in Paris, he was not blind to the limitations under which they worked. Nonetheless Prokofiev was not a man for limitations. At no point did he consider changing or amending his style or ideas to suit a particular audience. Despite continuous challenges, he remained true to his own understanding of what his authentic music should be and sound like.

5

The Search for a New Freedom

I stood and watched the sleighs careering
And listened to my native speech.
Anna Akhmatova[1]

Throughout his time in Europe, Prokofiev found he could not avoid
intersecting with geopolitics, where his music was often politicized,
reinterpreted and aligned with his physical as well as perceived
cultural locations. More frustratingly, he was trapped in a cycle
where his music and performances of his works were continuously
either out of time or behind time. The reasons for *Chout* not coming
to the stage until six years after its composition were not within his
control. But this holding pattern happened for so many of his other
works (such as *The Gambler*, *The Love for Three Oranges* and *Fiery
Angel*) that the composer was both vexed by and used to this pattern
of events.

Prokofiev was sincere about his desire to work with Soviet
ideas and materials, even though these kinds of materials were
not immediately clear or familiar to him. One might argue that
Prokofiev was writing in a style that was largely contrary to
anything being produced in Europe and America towards the end
of the 1920s. Nonetheless, he had great faith in his adaptability and
flexibility, qualities that had served him well in his musical career
so far. He spoke about this serious commitment to contemporary
composition in an article published in *Vechernaya Moskva* on
6 December 1932: 'What subject matter am I looking for? Not
caricatures of shortcomings, ridiculing the negative features of our

life. I am interested in subject matter that would assert the positive elements. The heroic aspects of socialist construction. The new man. The struggle to overcome obstacles.'[2] Even though Prokofiev was speaking in generalities, and before he had made official the decision to move, his words show a dedication to engaging with ideals of newness, which, for all we know, he might have assumed were connected to some aspects of modernity. He was soon to find out that not much could be further from the truth.

Moving back to the Soviet Union, where control and restraint was the order of the day, might well appear a paradoxical and regressive move. Prokofiev could not imagine or predict the extent to which interference by the state apparatus in his artistic endeavours would be present. Indeed, in the first few years he was allowed to work with relative artistic freedom. Scholars have argued that Prokofiev was tired of being second to Stravinsky in Paris and in Europe and second to Rachmaninov in America. But while this may have some truth to it, Prokofiev's intentions on returning to the Soviet Union were artistic as well as pragmatic. It is also highly likely that, given his single-minded focus on creativity, he found the mundane trappings of material daily life, and making a living, both draining and distracting. After a decade of battling in the West he was ready for change. Leningrad (as St Petersburg was known from 1924) and Moscow must have seemed appealing to him from that vantage point.

Katerina Clark argues that after 1930 Moscow, having been made the country's capital in 1917 following the Bolsheviks' relocation there from the Imperial capital of St Petersburg, became the centre of Soviet culture in two ways: first, most commissions and publications were emerging from Moscow and therefore the city was perceived as the locus of cultural activity and innovation. Intellectuals relocated to the city and new works were performed there. Second, she argues, culture tends to spread 'centripetally'. In other words, Moscow became the beacon that the rest of the country sought to emulate: 'the canon came largely from Moscow.'[3] This was applicable to most fields, including literature, architecture and, to a large extent, music. Composers were located in or, like

Prokofiev, brought to Moscow (Shostakovich being a notable exception). Moscow saw itself as the artistic leader for the new Soviet Union and held its artists to very specific standards.

One of the people tasked with trying to convince Prokofiev to make a permanent return to his homeland was the composer Lev Atovmyan. His assignment was to demonstrate how the Soviet Union could offer Prokofiev opportunities that colleagues in the West did not have access to. He repeatedly emphasized to Prokofiev that in the Soviet Union composers wrote specifically to paid commissions. Furthermore, Atovmyan argued, Prokofiev would retain copyright through this process, with additional fees payable on public performances as well as further royalties due from a publisher or a concert organization. An unassuming but loyal figure, in the end Atovmyan was instrumental to Prokofiev's success and material comfort on his return to the Soviet Union. Even during the composer's transitional period in France and the USSR, Atovmyan negotiated the contracts for *Lieutenant Kijé* and *Egyptian Nights*. The former was written to accompany the anti-tsar satire of 1927 written by Yury Tynyanov. The film director Alexander Fayntsimmer allowed Prokofiev freedom and creativity with his film music commission. Composed between 1933 and 1934 (although Prokofiev had been thinking about the medium of film since his trip

Sergei and Lina Prokofiev, with their sons Sviatoslav and Oleg, 1936.

Sergei, Lina and Oleg, 1936.

to the United States in 1930), the film was produced at Belgoskino Film Studio. Prokofiev created a five-movement suite from this score, which remains popular to this day, especially the penultimate Troika movement. The gently mocking and satirical story of the army officer who is brought into existence through a clerical error that is never rectified is a piece full of humour and warmth. With this work too, Prokofiev continued to focus on the inner world of each character, eschewing purely musical representations of them. He immersed himself in the creation of this film score, attending rehearsals and, as he had done with *The Gambler*, making notes for the actors. The final work was accessible, distinctively written and orchestrated and, very crucially, Russian sounding. It made Prokofiev a household name in the USSR and converted him into a sought-after composer for this medium too. As Kevin Bartig notes, in the final two decades of his life in the Soviet Union, Prokofiev was drawn into the excitement of developing the potential of music and technology in the film-making area.[4] He was offered around twenty film commissions, of which he completed eight.

On the composer's permanent return to his homeland, Atovmyan arranged Prokofiev's first set of contracts. In both cases he made sure the paperwork contained the relevant clauses for Prokofiev to retain the ability to terminate a contract if he was not content with how the agreement was playing out. Whether the composer would ever have been allowed to renege on a contract is doubtful; these were simply assurances designed to ensure that Prokofiev felt confident in his dealings with the new Soviet government. In his memoirs Atovmyan remembers Prokofiev saying to him, 'I am now convinced that in the Soviet Union there are wonderful opportunities for creative activity and, I suppose, there actually is no reason for me to go on torturing myself endlessly with border crossings just to give concerts.'[5] The combination of pragmatic thinking alongside the creative enterprise never deserted the composer.

Within this context, the relocation of Prokofiev to the Soviet Union was and is instantly prone to politicization. For the Soviet Union and its cultural leaders, acquiring assets from Europe designated the USSR's new culture as equal to (if much younger than) the traditions of European intellectualism. In building its own culture from its pre-Soviet ruins, during the 1930s the USSR also appropriated trends from other countries, including the United States and Western European nations. Katerina Clark refers to this as the 'Great Appropriation'.[6] In her words, in the Soviet Union cultural dominance was pursued systematically and insistently because 'culture was power.'[7] The 'country developed as a singular "civilization" but did so while simultaneously interacting with the outside world, and primarily with continental Europe' and the United States, the former being 'the main sphere of interest for social Soviet intellectuals, though with America as well'.[8] The possibility of participating in the creation and framing of a new musical aesthetic for Russia no doubt appealed to Prokofiev, who saw his mission as a composer as one of leadership as well as creation.

A number of compositions bridge the period around 1931–5, when Prokofiev was still based in Europe but was looking ahead, psychologically if not yet practically, to his move back to the USSR.

On these projects, Prokofiev was working with the most distinguished and innovative artists of the period, so it is no wonder that these years brought him great artistic satisfaction and a renewed vigour and belief in his art. Projects include *Romeo and Juliet, Lieutenant Kijé,* Symphonic Song (op. 57) and *Egyptian Nights.* This was an attempt to combine Bernard Shaw's *Caesar and Cleopatra,* first produced in 1906, with Shakespeare's *Antony and Cleopatra.* To this was added a monologue from the poem 'Egyptian Nights' by Pushkin, from which the project derived its title. It was produced by the Moscow Kamerny Theatre, staged by its renowned director and co-founder Alexander Tairov, whose wife, Alisa Koonen, took the title role. Just as he had done with *Lieutenant Kijé,* Prokofiev was loath to waste the work and time he had spent on *Egyptian Nights,* and so he created a suite from the work to ensure it had a life outside the theatre.

Prokofiev started work on *Romeo and Juliet* in November 1934 while on another trip to the USSR. He drafted the scenario with the influential director Sergei Radlov, who was a friend and had directed *The Love for Three Oranges.*[9] On this project too, the composer was working with another leading contemporary theatre director. Unsurprisingly this scenario needed to go through several drafts in response to feedback coming from different sources. Given the composer's now-habitual processes for creating ballets, where he tended to take the lead on most (if not all) the dramaturgical decisions, including scenarios, one wonders how the composer reacted to this more collaborative approach to creating an artwork. It would seem that Prokofiev tolerated this feature of collaborative work in the Soviet Union, in the spirit of the time, especially since he considered that he was working with theatre experts of the highest calibre. In the early years following his return, the composer received multiple commissions, including incidental music and music for state events. He was tasked with working with various artists, so he seems to have been content with this arrangement; he may have indeed been reminded of the early Diaghilev days.

Nonetheless, it is difficult to imagine how he envisaged this kind of benevolent 'guidance' – which he saw as interference – would

Sergei Prokofiev and Nikolai Myaskovsky in Moscow, 1941.

work in the future. Perhaps at the time he preferred not to think about it. However, given that very few people were ever allowed to see his work in progress (the few that were included Myaskovsky, Diaghilev, Stravinsky and Dukelsky), let alone critique it, it would only be a matter of time until he began to chafe under the mediocrity of well-meaning suggestions. Although he might not have said anything much about it at the time (except directly to his collaborators, who subsequently found this attitude quite difficult to work with), it is clear in his letters to friends like Myaskovsky that Prokofiev merely tolerated this intrusion with dark humour and sarcasm. As his connections with Soviet contacts deepened, he maintained relationships with American friends and benefactors, such as Ephraim Gottlieb. In a letter to him dated 31 May 1936, the composer spoke of his wife and sons as having arrived in Moscow a fortnight earlier. At this point he was still waiting for his furniture and the piano to arrive. He discussed his compositions for children, a trend which was, as he explained to his friend, very fashionable at the time. In addition, he referred to the Pushkin centenary works (scores planned for the play *Eugene Onegin* and the unrealized 1937 film *The Queen of Spades*). Prokofiev was unable to send money out from the USSR to the United States to pay an outstanding fee to his American managers, but Gottlieb took care of that for him.

Commissions for theatrical works, in the form of incidental music to accompany plays produced to celebrate the Pushkin centenary, came flowing in before Prokofiev had made the decision to relocate. One could cynically argue that these commissions were only offered to him to lure him back, enticing him with better artistic prospects in the Soviet Union. But that would only be part of the picture. Prokofiev was a highly prized artistic asset, and one who could easily take his place alongside Shostakovich as a major composer of the USSR.

Although the doctrine of Socialist Realism in the arts was in its infancy, it must already have been clear to the cultural commissars of the Soviet Union that their musical scene could do with the injection of some glamour and international credibility. Whether that approach could ever be sustained was another matter entirely.

Sergei Prokofiev, Dmitri Shostakovich and Aram Khachaturian, 1945.

Prokofiev would be able to provide both in equal measure, at least in his first decade in the USSR. To Western eyes, on a Soviet-sanctioned concert tour with Lina, the Prokofievs appeared a glamorous couple content with the life they had in the Soviet Union. Alice Berezovsky, the wife of the Russian émigré composer Nikolai Berezovsky, remembers the occasion when she first met Prokofiev and Lina, who were being hosted in the United States by their longtime, steadfast friends and former Parisian neighbours Natalia and Serge Koussevitzky in January 1937. Alice's impressions of 'Madame Prokofiev', as she referred to her, clearly show that the Prokofievs appeared to understand their unspoken deal with the Soviet state.[10] The children attended a private English-language school in Russia and the composer had the use of a Rolls-Royce. In attendance at a concert by the Boston Symphony, Lina impressed with 'her exquisitely cut, shimmering lamé evening dress. In her hair, around her neck, and on her arms and fingers she wore a set of enormous antique topazes . . . designed by a jeweler in Paris.'[11] By all outward appearances it seemed as if Prokofiev and his wife were leading the lives of expatriates within the Soviet Union in a way that would be eventually unsustainable. While Lina would have been more than comfortable mingling in those social circles as an expat,

Prokofiev, never quite comfortable in such social spaces anyway, would take the opportunity to retreat. Scholars have suggested that as long as the composer was able to travel abroad, he and his wife were willing to turn a blind eye to what was or may have been going on around them. Or at least they knew enough not to probe by asking too many questions and to accept at face value the responses provided by the state with regard to the treatment of various figures. Certainly, observing the Prokofievs at close quarters during this period would have made a significant impression not only on their Moscow friends and acquaintances, but on the émigrés who hosted them on their overseas tours. Some of Prokofiev's ability to paint a rosy picture or rely on selective memory can also be perceived in his correspondence and communication with the younger composer Dukelsky, with whom Prokofiev continued to have a genuine relationship even after his repatriation to the USSR.

As we have already seen, in Prokofiev's early years, and then in his years abroad, he was an artist who loved the theatre. He delighted in writing for the stage; he loved creating characters, playing with storylines and using the text to pursue his preference for declamation. Theatre was Prokofiev's greatest passion, manifested initially in – as it was to be throughout his life – his operatic works. All this was well-established by the time he had completed *The Gambler*. That fervour for the theatre was never to leave him, even though he had scant opportunity to pursue it in the late 1920s. No doubt this caused him concern and discontent, even if it was never explicitly articulated in public or to his friends. Thus when commissions started coming in from the Soviet Union, which allowed him to entertain the possibility of writing music for the stage once again, Prokofiev was predictably both excited and reluctant to let anything get in the way of these opportunities. Regardless of whether officials of the Soviet government were simply being canny in offering these kinds of opportunities to further encourage his move back to the USSR, Prokofiev was thrilled by these new events.

While the composer was travelling and making his final preparations to relocate to the Soviet Union, the now-infamous *Pravda* editorial entitled 'Chaos Instead of Music' appeared on

28 January 1936. The article criticized Shostakovich's opera *Lady Macbeth of the Mtsensk District*, arguing that it was 'an intentionally discordant flood of sounds. Embryos of musical phrases drown, tear away, and disappear again in the din, grinding and squealing.' Although Prokofiev did not make public mention of this editorial that had consequences not simply for Shostakovich but for music across the USSR, he gave it serious consideration in private. Atovmyan reported that Prokofiev asked to see a copy of the piano and orchestral scores of *Lady Macbeth*, which were procured for him, and when Prokofiev returned them some days later he declared his appreciation for the opera's dramaturgy and scenic construction. He also thought the orchestration was inventive and asked for his opinions to be conveyed to Shostakovich. It is typical of Prokofiev that he would first analyse the music on its own terms before accepting the judgement professed so devastatingly on the Soviet Union's most prominent composer. After examining the music, however, he must have realized that the infamous article had nothing to do with the quality of Shostakovich's music.

Ultimately, Prokofiev seems to have concluded that he was immune to this kind of criticism, given the effort that the Soviet government had gone to to bring him back. But it did not escape his wife Lina, who was concerned enough to discuss this at home (while still in Paris) and in correspondence. Suvchinsky appears to have advised Lina to rethink their decision to return to the Soviet Union. He pointed her to some further *Pravda* articles that would be of interest to her because they demonstrated the falsity of some of the claims being made by the cultural regime at the time. Eventually, however, she was in support of her husband's move to the Soviet Union, even if it was with some trepidation and reservations, and probably more caution than her husband. In another letter to Prokofiev, she argued, 'It seems to me that in all of this drama you can play a very important role, but only, of course, with great tact, and without creating any unnecessary enemies.'[12]

The die was cast, and Prokofiev relocated to the Soviet Union on 20 March 1936. He had arrived ahead of his family and was living in a hotel on Red Square while waiting for his permanent domicile to be made available to him. He had been promised an apartment in Moscow that would house himself and his children. A couple of months later, Lina arrived in Moscow with the two boys. They stayed for a little while in the same hotel before moving to their first apartment five weeks later.

It is impossible to understand Lina Prokofiev's situation on her return to the Soviet Union. Certainly, she supported the composer in his decision to return, although this was only after much discussion, disagreement and consideration of the situation. Prokofiev expected Lina would integrate into Soviet society, however, her assimilation was far from seamless because her upbringing was sophisticated and cosmopolitan. She would stand out from Soviet women not simply by the clothes she wore or how she carried herself, but by her interests, her experiences living and working in other countries, as well as her ability to function in several languages. Nonetheless, she had always expected that both her and her husband would be able to sustain an artistic career in the Soviet Union while maintaining their overseas and Western connections. They intended to continue taking advantage of the generously remunerated American tours that Prokofiev's Western promoters organized for him.

However, these tours and their physical distance put a strain on the marriage, and with this estrangement from Prokofiev, Lina came under much closer scrutiny by Soviet authorities. Although her activities were monitored, she found creative ways to continue to mingle in foreign embassies and attend events such as film screenings; she befriended attachés and sought, often by subterfuge, to keep alive memories of a previous life that would have now seemed surreal to her. These moments kept her going and were worth every effort she made to maintain them.

Leaving Lina to figure out the best role for herself in this new context, Prokofiev busied himself in an almost unending stream of work and commissions. Among these were *Romeo and Juliet*, the *Cantata for the Twentieth Anniversary of the October Revolution*, mass songs and a set of children's pieces for piano. At this time, too, centenaries of key artistic figures like Shakespeare and Pushkin, for example, were being celebrated in the USSR and such celebrations normally led to lucrative state commissions for composers. One of the reasons why Prokofiev was willing to put up with interference in his work was that he was able to collaborate on commissions with the finest theatrical directors of the day.

While Prokofiev threw himself into his new Soviet reality, fashioning the right environments to enable his continued creative productivity, the West had not forgotten about him. His Soviet minders were sufficiently content to let him undertake some foreign tours as part of a soft propaganda push promoting life in the Soviet Union. Now that Prokofiev had made the decision to move back to the homeland, his last performing years in the West provoked a number of strong statements from critics. The implication was that his status was now beyond question: Prokofiev had an 'inborn instinct for classicism' along with 'a certain amount of remorselessness' in his 'methods'.[13] Rollo H. Myers discussed the composer in a detailed article in October 1936, characterizing his music as 'still primarily a healthy exercise, a form of intellectual gymnastics'. The critic observed that the composer wrote

> to give pleasure; his conception of music is that it should be a recreation and a relaxation, not a matter for solemn meditation or soul revealing 'self-expression' . . . Being Russian, too, Prokofiev must have felt the danger of this hot-house atmosphere more acutely . . . Hence the clean, clear-cut rhythms, simple tunes, and brutal unsophisticated harmonies [that] mark all his early work, and which later are trimmed and put to the services of a direct musical speech, full of dynamic energy and a virile expression of healthy animal spirits and joie de vivre.[14]

Other accolades from important contemporary composers included one from Georges Auric, who also considered Prokofiev one of the most brilliant contemporary pianists.

> Although he is essentially a Russian composer, we must not expect from him today the sort of more or less brilliant variations

based on Slav folk-lore to which so many works, whose names are familiar to us all, owe their success . . . I admire the way in which Prokofiev at his best preserves his equilibrium in the midst of aesthetic problems of all kinds, since, thanks to his magnificently natural creative gift, he has no need to worry about them.[15]

Auric understood that Prokofiev composed Russian music on his own terms, an approach that much contemporary critical reception found difficult to comprehend. In 1937 British critics called Prokofiev 'Russian without being proletarian', by which they presumably meant that he continued to write music of a sufficiently complex standard while retaining Russian-sounding motifs, intervallic patterns and harmonic structures.[16] By 1938 the argument about his 'greatness' seemed more of a moot point. After relinquishing his more active connections with the West and returning to his homeland, critics began to eulogize him ahead of his time: 'Prokofiev, as we all know, is one of the two leaders of the neo-classical movement, and it was fitting that the evening should begin with his famous Classical Symphony.'[17] (In this evening concert Prokofiev was the 'distinguished guest-conductor' of the BBC symphony concert at Queen's Hall in a concert dedicated to his music. It included first performances of Violin Concerto No. 2 with Robert Soetens as a soloist, alongside Prokofiev on the piano, and the suite from his ballet *Romeo and Juliet*.)

Others focus on his consummate skill in orchestration, still recognizing the enfant terrible: 'Two extracts from an opera by Prokofiev, one of Russia's irrepressibles, proved vastly entertaining, their pert wittiness being underlined by orchestration of a peculiar dryness of timbre, quite exhilarating as a relief from conventionality.'[18] Despite his renewed connection to his motherland, now a Soviet confederation, Prokofiev continued to follow international press and was irritated by the reaction some of his works elicited. He sought to control the narrative enough to engage in a conversation about what he saw as blatant mischaracterizations of his music. In 1932, for instance, he wrote to the critic Watson Lyle, peevishly observing:

I expected your article to be the first serious study on my music after all the nonsense written up to now in England about it; but I see that you had to limit yourself to a kind of drawing-room chat . . . I did not tell you 'Music without emotion? But it is not possible'. The very word 'emotion' I asked you to use with caution; otherwise you will make your readers believe that a new Puccini is born.[19]

This uneasy relationship with the press lasted a lifetime; Prokofiev was to take the lessons he learnt in these contexts to the Soviet Union.

The summer of 1936 continued to be a very fruitful one for Prokofiev. On his return to the Soviet Union, he also turned his attention to writing music for children. There was a push from above to encourage composers to create suitable works for a younger generation. With the composer's quintessential understanding of sound combinations, as well as of the challenges of piano playing, it was inevitable that he would write classics that remain in the repertoire of young pianists today. These include his collection of pieces for piano, op. 65, which demonstrates his continued love for transparent textures, suggestive of fairy-tale imagery. Crisp textures and rhythmic humour make these works vintage Prokofiev and beloved by children worldwide. *Peter and the Wolf* remains a children's classic to this day. As usual he wrote the text on his own, only on occasion consulting Natalia Satz, the director of the Moscow Children's Theatre. This work allowed Prokofiev to immerse himself in the magic of childhood and in the pure delight of instrumentation and orchestration. The plot refers to folk traditions, although the character of Peter in the tale is a contemporary Young Pioneer.[20] Prokofiev worked on this piece with alacrity and pleasure; it proved to be an instant hit with children. Concurrently the composer worked on the Russian Overture, which included folk-inspired motifs and recalls elements of the Ballets Russes.

In these later and more reflective years, the legacy and accessibility of his music, along with the quality of both aesthetic and final product, became Prokofiev's primary concern. The arguments he used in rationalizing his thinking had echoes from a previous period in his life, when he had passionately debated and advocated for the genre of opera as a valid twentieth-century model of music, despite opposition from other strong-minded characters like Stravinsky and Diaghilev. What Prokofiev was not prepared for were the serious reprisals arising from what he would have considered normal and routine bureaucratic processes of the period. His first real experience of the state meddling in his work came with the composition of *Cantata for the Twentieth Anniversary of the October Revolution*. The contract for this work dates from 26 June 1935; it states that the work was intended for radio broadcast. Initially Prokofiev designed the work as a tribute to Lenin but over time it evolved into a ten-movement structure that moves from the revolution to the civil war and Stalin's pledge to Lenin as well as the Soviet Constitution. It was a bald statement on the part of the composer to demonstrate where his loyalties lay. The work had a rather complicated evolution. Prokofiev approached the writing of this cantata in the same way that he did with previous works; in other words, he turned to the original words of Marx, Lenin and Stalin for direct inspiration and appropriate text-setting. The composer must have thought that as he had successfully and meaningfully worked with text in this way on numerous occasions, his approach to these key Soviet texts would be appreciated and not that far off from what was required.

But Prokofiev eventually came to realize that he was trapped in a complex and contradictory situation; not only because what was enshrined in policy could not be interpreted to the letter, but because Soviet culture had constantly moving goalposts. Prokofiev asked an old friend, Boris Demchinsky, for help with the libretto – although the writer was hesitant, his feedback was honest and helpful to the composer. Demchinsky was of the opinion, when he eventually responded to Prokofiev's plea for help, that the composer should apply a broad-brush approach to the revolution that led to the establishment of communism, rather than trying to be pedantically accurate with dates and words. In his view it was critical to focus

Sergei Prokofiev conducting, *c.* 1934.

on the concepts of brotherhood of peoples and emphasize the happy Soviet life. Excessive detail would distract from the cantata's essential spirit of victory and happy reflection. Demchinsky also advised Prokofiev to include the 1818 Pushkin poem 'To Chaadayev', and pointed the composer to the actual words that should be included. These would help synthesize the entire work and provide cohesion both in narrative and in symbolism.

Prokofiev would have appreciated Demchinsky's timely helping hand, but the latter did not in the end provide the assistance that was needed within the required timeframe. The frustrated composer was compelled to figure out his own textual outline for the work. The first draft of the vocal score was completed on 5 June 1937 but Prokofiev continued to work on orchestration until September of that year. What ensued was a complicated revision process during which the cantata was critiqued for containing incomprehensible music, with the result that eventually the work remained unperformed. Thanks to a surge in Prokofiev scholarship, we now have evidence that the composer was caught up in a settling of scores within the bureaucratic elements of the regime, the inevitable result of which was that the conductor (not Prokofiev) was quietly instructed not to rehearse the work.[21] But Prokofiev took a rational approach to the process and continued to expect a premiere even a year later. In the meantime, while this torturous process unfolded, the composer had written another work, *Songs of Our Days*, which he called a 'different, somewhat simpler piece'.[22]

Nonetheless, despite maintaining a positive facade, the setback unsettled Prokofiev, who had after all approached the work with great sincerity, utilizing established methods from his past compositional processes. As far as he was concerned, he was making every effort to be authentic with the texts and to respond musically, without compromising his compositional approach, to the important precepts of Socialist Realism – at least as he understood them from the limited time he had been back in his homeland. The composer was caught within the infighting of the cultural bureaucracy – not all members of the music division were pleased to see Prokofiev back. Some, who were minor composers themselves, felt threatened by his prodigious gifts and attempted to put obstacles in his way, or, at least, went out of their way to not support him. Prokofiev, with his brash and insensitive manner, did not suffer fools lightly (at least in the first few years of his return) and did not help the situation. He was direct, critical and dismissive, always wanting those around him to adhere to the standards that he had set for himself. The people he was working with, however, had neither his colossal experience nor his international perspective on contemporary music, and it was easier for them to characterize him as lacking in understanding of Soviet principles. It was a simple charge for them to levy at him and one he could not ever persuasively refute.

Given Prokofiev's disappointing operatic career to date (none of his four operas were yet established in the operatic repertory), he turned eagerly to the challenge of writing a stage commission. Theatre was a highly regarded art form in the Soviet Union and with Prokofiev's early experience of the theatre and poetry in the pre-revolutionary days, he turned his energies to these projects with alacrity and vigour. At no point would he have imagined that commissions would go unperformed, and no amount of foresight could have prepared him for that eventuality.

Prokofiev scored the incidental music for four plays across a four-year period. He approached writing for the genre with his normal mixture of attention to detail and pragmatism, noting in an interview in 1936 that he rarely accepted a commission without first familiarizing himself with the full text of the play. His approach to collaboration was perhaps surprisingly relaxed, preferring to receive clear instructions from the playwright and the director. In a pithy comment, he noted that it is helpful to have specific instructions: 'Here I need a minute and a quarter of music' or 'give me something tender and melancholy here.'[23] But he was also sensitive to the programmatic aspects of composing, noting that drama theatres do not normally have the right acoustics for orchestral forces:

> It happens that while voices sound well from the stage, the orchestra is either too loud or too soft, or both. In drama theatres orchestras tend to be dreadfully noisy and one waits impatiently for the music to cease. This is often due not only to the acoustics, which have not taken music into account, but to the 'quantity and quality' of the orchestra itself.[24]

The advice that Prokofiev shared with composers is valuable: one must familiarize oneself with the theatres that one is writing for, and watch new productions with a view to understanding the available forces in order to 'achieve a smooth, not too harsh *forte* in any orchestra, and also a *pianissimo* that will not interfere with the voices of the actors, especially if the orchestra can be placed under the stage, behind a screen or in the wings'.[25]

The first of these scores was *Boris Godunov*. This project reunited Vsevolod Meyerhold as director and Prokofiev as composer for the first time since their collaboration on *Three Oranges*. The original intention was to stage this play as part of the Pushkin centennial celebration of 1937. Meyerhold had radical plans for the drama, which had been discussed with Prokofiev and which the composer was excited about. However, the political situation in 1937 was such that any narrative about leaders and their legitimacy was dangerous; a historical drama about a tsar ascending to the throne

Vsevolod Meyerhold and Sergei Prokofiev, date unknown.

by murdering the legitimate heirs was doubly so. Indeed, the play
was removed from the repertory of the Moscow Art Theatre on
the orders of Vyacheslav Molotov, then Chairman of the Council
of People's Commissars. Meyerhold had been interested in *Boris
Godunov* for quite a while. More than two decades earlier, in 1911,
he had participated in a production of the play at the Mariinsky
Theatre in St Petersburg. Meyerhold had also rehearsed the play
in 1924 for a projected staging in Moscow, which had to be shelved
because of problems with casting. So, by 1934, Meyerhold had given
this work a great deal of thought and, being the intelligent director
that he was, had planned it to be a critique of the current leadership.
The rehearsal transcripts show how Meyerhold wanted energetic
and muscular acting, intending to eliminate the barriers between
auditorium and stage. When Meyerhold asked Prokofiev to write
the incidental music, he gave instructions that the score should have
an element of the diabolic. Accordingly, the composer introduced
drunken singing, ballroom dancing, choruses and songs. He used
rhythm to further create a disjunction between and among the
onstage characters themselves. Aside from the dance scenes, which

included a polonaise and mazurka, there was also a quick and swiftly composed battle scene.

It is hardly surprising that by the time Meyerhold came to restage *Boris Godunov* using the modernist approaches to the theatre that he had developed, it would be a dangerous enterprise, especially as he intended to criticize Stalin by implication. Prokofiev played a run-through of his music to some of the actors on 16 November 1936. It appears that his score was enthusiastically received and Meyerhold was impressed by the direct approach of the music. This score, as he saw it, brought together the sentiment of Pushkin with the declamation of Mussorgsky.

Eugene Onegin, the second score following *Boris Godunov*, was the composer's opportunity to re-engage with his beloved Russian literature and simultaneously to respond to Tchaikovsky's own setting of *Onegin*. Prokofiev wrote about this in an article for *Vechernyaya Moskva* dated 22 June 1936. Here he spoke of the importance of capturing what he calls 'the true spirit of Pushkin'. This approach was in keeping with the composer's own understanding of realism and authenticity on the stage, developed through declamation, theatrical rhythm and scenographic plasticity – all ideas developed during his work with Meyerhold decades earlier on *The Gambler*. He would also have responded positively to Tairov's plan to create a dramatic enactment. Sigizmund Krzhizhanovsky, a contemporary writer, was to set the Pushkin text for this project.[26] But Krzhizhanovsky's adaptation came under significant criticism for his unorthodox approach to the original Pushkin: for example, he reconfigured the order of the scenes and made several changes to the philosophical and literary asides. This would have been immediately noticeable to a Russian audience and would no doubt have irked the official censors, who were looking for pedestrian and unsophisticated approaches to Pushkin's text.

Perhaps the most obvious change was the replacement of the narrator with others who speak in the first person. Prokofiev saw the logic in the adaptation and proceeded to compose music based on the draft that he had seen. But when the adaptation was sent to Glavrepertkom, a commission set up to approve new music

Meyerhold and Prokofiev, date unknown.

and performer's repertoires, it was not approved.[27] Tairov was extremely distressed by the outcome of this official review and urged Krzhizhanovsky to rework and address the comments made by the adjudication panel. Prokofiev was largely not involved in these discussions. His task, as he saw it, was to wait for what he thought were artistic issues to be resolved and then to adjust his music in accordance with the final draft. This would not have been a difficult thing for him to do because it was a working method that he was used to. He created a distinct musical characterization for each of the main characters in the play and he was able to use a number of other musical approaches to suggest different soundscapes, enabling the music to delineate and support the events unfolding on stage. In this way Prokofiev's music rose above the text, remaining adaptable and flexible so that it could be set to the final scenario and script regardless of any variations and amendments it needed to undergo.

In August 1937, Prokofiev was asked to compose incidental music for a production of Shakespeare's *Hamlet*. Directed by Sergei

Radlov, this staging took place at the Leningrad Academic Theatre of Drama. Prokofiev would have been aware of the circumstances surrounding a recent production of the play by Nikolai Akimov in 1932. This was a famously controversial production in which Ophelia was characterized as an inebriated prostitute and Hamlet as a comedian. Only the music of Shostakovich was above criticism.[28] Within this context, it is unsurprising that when Radlov came to stage *Hamlet*, he wanted to represent the main character as a force for action. Radlov gave Prokofiev specific instructions that were seemingly paradoxical: he asked the composer to create ghost music but without creating anything mystical. He also asked him to compose shorter folk songs for Ophelia. The reason that Radlov instructed the composer to avoid mystical music was because this was not in keeping with the aesthetics of the time. At the time of this commission, Prokofiev was also working on the orchestration for the *Cantata for the Twentieth Anniversary of the October Revolution*; during autumn 1937 he began work on *Hamlet*. However, this was a challenging process because he ended up not completing *Hamlet* until February 1938, when he was on his way to the United States for his final tour. The orchestration itself was a logistical problem and Prokofiev had to enlist the help of his assistant Pavel Lamm to orchestrate the work.

The music was precisely what Radlov needed. It is written in ten numbers, an approach that Prokofiev used increasingly in works written during this later period. In a contemporary interview, he explained that when it came to writing the musical accompaniment for the shadow of Hamlet's father there was no mysticism 'because Shakespeare himself intended none'. There was also no need 'to convey the horror felt by the actors or the spectators of the appearance of the ghost. The music here should convey the emotions of the wrong father appearing from the outer darkness to rouse his son to avenge his murder.'[29] Unlike *Boris Godunov* and *Eugene Onegin*, *Hamlet* did reach the stage and it was a success, perhaps filling the gap left by Akimov's *Hamlet*. The composer himself attended rehearsals as well as performances; for once he was able to see the triumphant success of one of his theatrical works.

Prokofiev was certainly genuine in his desire to participate fully in the cultural life of the Soviet Union. He explained some of his ideas in press articles of the time. He wrote about the importance of the symphonic form, referring to Myaskovsky's Sixteenth Symphony, which he praised for its beauty of material and compositional mastery, arguing that it was 'a true work of art that does not strive for external effects or seek to curry favour with the public'.[30] These early pronouncements by Prokofiev in the press are for the most part genuine because he wasn't used to having to censor himself; he came to the Soviet Union thinking that he would be allowed to preserve his artistic freedom and would also be expected to demonstrate some leadership in developing music for the new Soviet state. Prokofiev took his duties seriously and somewhat to the letter. Even when speaking about the role of music for the masses, he was articulate without compromising on his own ideas, stating that young composers need not indulge audiences to retain their attention. In his own words, 'pandering always has an element of insincerity about it and nothing good ever came of that. The masses want great music.' Urging young composers to maintain their standards, he argued that audiences 'understand far more than some composers think and they want to deepen their understanding'.[31]

Prokofiev had always wanted to write accessible music. One of the main problems that he initially had with Diaghilev and the argument surrounding modernism was precisely around the accessibility and comprehensibility of his artistic voice. He abhorred artifice and convoluted ways of expressing essential musical ideas. Therefore, it is no surprise that in urging a younger generation of Soviet composers, Prokofiev would return to the ideals that he had himself espoused throughout his life. This was not all the composer had to say about Soviet music. Perhaps he felt the need to speak clearly about his mission and to ensure that his ideas were understood by those who were in control of censorship. After all, he already had significant experience of the press misreading and misrepresenting his work.

There is compelling evidence in Russian archives that Prokofiev was not the naive incognizant that some commentators in the West, including Stravinsky, made him out to be. Incomplete jottings in his personal papers reveal his understanding of the role of the composer in the Soviet state, noting the importance of elevating music for the masses, rather than reducing it to what he considered to be unsophisticated music.[32] His opinion of contemporary Soviet composers was not complimentary. In his notes he refers to the music of the composer and administrator Ivan Dzerzhinsky as illiterate.[33] When Prokofiev came to write a series of articles for public consumption, this directness was nuanced, but in his unpublished notes, he never compromised with the truth. In a draft article, he observed that the concept of Formalism in music had been far too zealously espoused, with the result that composers had given up on searching for new material, in case that process was glibly labelled Formalism. As he succinctly put it, if composers were working with second-rate material, the music could not be first-rate. These notes were never made public, so perhaps he shared them, or preliminary drafts of them, with friends, who dissuaded him from submitting anything for publication written in such a direct and abrasive tone. But the real and uncompromising Prokofiev can be easily recognised in these thoughts.

In an article in *Pravda* in 1937, Prokofiev spoke about the search for a musical idiom worthy of Socialism. With his characteristic penchant for hitting the nail on the head, but with a more muted tone, he argued,

the search for a musical idiom . . . is a worthy but difficult task for the composer. Music in our country has become the heritage of vast masses of people. Their artistic taste and demands are growing with amazing speed. And this is something the Soviet composer must take into account in each new work.

It is something like shooting at a moving target . . . That is why I consider it a mistake for a composer to strive for simplification. Any attempt to 'play down' to the listener is a subconscious underestimation of his cultural maturity and the development of his tastes; such an attempt has an element of insincerity. And music that is insincere cannot be enduring.[34]

He noted that in his own work he had striven for 'clarity and melodiousness' while at the same time he 'scrupulously avoided palming off familiar harmonies and tunes'. The challenge, he argued, lies in 'composing clear, straightforward music'. As Prokofiev stated, 'the clarity must be new, not old.'[35] Given the intensity of the ideas expressed in this article, especially within the context of what we know about Prokofiev's ideas about artistic integrity, none of these thoughts appear disingenuous. Certainly, he may have been playing down the role of innovation in his work in favour of a more elaborate form of lyricism. Nonetheless, there is real integrity in his utterances from this early period in the Soviet Union.

Once Prokofiev had, to some extent at least, settled in the artistic ways of the Soviet Union, his thoughts turned to opera, a genre never far from his thoughts. Predictably, he set himself the highest standards – his aim was to compose an opera in a style that was both fluid and elevated in musical language and form, with renewed focus on his melodic approach. In devising this new Soviet opera, Prokofiev was not about to make any allowances for himself by resting on the laurels of his international reputation; neither was he about to renege on the dramaturgical principles he had espoused for the previous two decades. In an interview from the period, he articulated these ideas very clearly to a new Soviet public, sharing with them that

> to write an opera on a Soviet theme is by no means a simple task
> . . . I had long wanted to write a Soviet opera, but I hesitated to
> undertake the job until I had a clear idea of how to approach
> the task. Besides, it was not easy to find a plot. I did not want
> a commonplace, static, trivial plot or, on the contrary, a plot
> that pointed too obvious a moral. I wanted live flesh and blood
> human beings with human passions, love, hatred, joy and sorrow
> arising naturally from the new conditions.[36]

One of the most compelling features of Prokofiev's pronouncements is his honesty about his artistic plans. He was not intending to cut corners with this opera and he similarly expected his audience to be equally demanding of their artists. In the above comment, he references the concept of the Soviet plot or narrative, which would need to be deployed in order for an artistic product to be categorized and accepted as Soviet. The composer demonstrated his continued commitment to reality on stage, still drawn from the theatre, and still having the audience's reaction and interaction at its heart. His interest in characterization, and in depicting and delineating those characters in the best possible way, remained intact. Prokofiev, at least at this stage, saw that Soviet opera could be a natural progression of the ideals he had explored in his first four operas. What is also surprising, given the fact that this article was written in 1940 (albeit not published until the late 1950s) is that so much of what he expresses in this piece echoes his 1916 article. For example, there too he noted that an opera should not have any static moments, while set pieces had no place in contemporary operas. In 1940, contrary to his previously expressed antagonism to set-pieces, Prokofiev now argued that the aria 'has a legitimate place in opera; it enables the composer to develop a broad melody and gives the singer an opportunity to display his vocal talents.'[37]

In his early pre-revolutionary public pronouncements, the composer would insist, with an interdisciplinary and modern outlook, that theatrical and acting skills were indispensable for a singer. While he might still have believed that, in this instance he thought it more prudent to focus on talent. Prokofiev made a distinction between two kinds of arias: one in which the action is static and nothing happens and the other containing more of an opportunity for an evolution of emotion within it. He also noted that he would avoid 'recitative', calling it 'the least interesting element in opera'. This is the other concession that Prokofiev made to his vision, and it was in response to previous criticism that considered his use of declamation not artistically appropriate. Indeed, he openly stated that 'at the more emotional moments I have tried to make the recitative melodious, producing a sort of receipt of melody and used rhythmic speech . . . for the more matter-of-fact parts.'[38] Here a seasoned and pragmatic Prokofiev revisited and tweaked his operatic aesthetic for the benefit of his new audiences. With the instinct of a practiced artistic entrepreneur, he managed his audiences' expectations and attempted to frame the opera to be as close to Socialist Realism as he was able to make it at that time. This document illuminates the composer's understanding of Socialism as he understood it at that point in his career.

For his first opera written in the Soviet Union, Prokofiev turned to a 1938 novella by Valentin Katayev titled *I am the Son of the Working People*. Katayev was a successful and politically engaged writer who had been involved in politics from an early age, fighting in the First World War and then in the Russian Civil War; his knowledge of the battlefield and his political insights were drawn from lived experience. He was not immune to criticism from the state, having been attacked in 1928 by the Russian Association of Proletarian Writers for anti-Soviet elements in his writing. Although it might have seemed as though the collaboration between Katayev and Prokofiev had a good chance of success, in the end they were an uneven match; besides, the composer had not collaborated with anyone this closely since his Diaghilev days. Katayev intended to adapt the novel to create a script for Prokofiev that would contain versified text for arias and set-pieces. But the composer had other ideas, declaring quite laconically that there would be no need for this, and that the text as it stood would suffice for him. The opera was entitled *Semyon Kotko* rather than the novel's longer title, demonstrating Prokofiev's continued preference for telling stories that are focused on the individual and their unique experience, rather than the collective.

Katayev's source novel was a romantic story that synthesized folk literature with Gogol's writings and therefore operated in several genres simultaneously. Prokofiev was adept at shifting between genres in a single work, exploiting the comic and the tragic as well as the Soviet narrative. In *Semyon Kotko* the storyline focused, at least in the composer's view, on two central concepts in storytelling: love and war, both themes eminently suitable for turning into an opera.[39] Some of the larger-scale scenes, such as the fire scene in Act III, are a powerful combination of the dramatic and the personal, bringing together his most compelling compositional tools to musically depict the unmitigated horrors of war. Prokofiev also did his best to root these characters in local colour and imagination. He took his research seriously, painstakingly looking for musical material that could function as pseudo-folk music. This was possibly his first real attempt to integrate a more focused sound in his writing by researching it. As Prokofiev had stated on many previous occasions, he always preferred creating his own individual material, even though he might have taken inspiration from other genres. Here the composer used folk material only for imitation and reference. The composer Dmitri Kabalevsky remembers Prokofiev advising him to 'take some folk tune and develop it as you would your own'.[40] This is exactly how he approached folk material: he did not condone or accept wholesale integration of real folk songs into his style. In his view, his role as a composer was to be inspired by the original folk material and then mediate and integrate it into his own score, rooted in a personal artistic voice.

As he continued to grapple with the essence of Soviet music and what it might be, Prokofiev found himself in the unenviable and acutely distressing position of needing to praise Stalin in such works as *Zdravitsa*, 'Hail to Stalin', a toast for Stalin on his sixtieth birthday. But even as he praised the leader of the USSR he was simultaneously unable to ignore the fate of close colleagues like the theatre director Meyerhold, who had suffered the ultimate price for his commitment to art.[41] Despite any misgivings he might have had, the ode to Stalin was deemed acceptable. *Zdravitsa* was first performed in Moscow on 21 December 1939. Prokofiev's son Oleg remembered that it was broadcast on loudspeakers to be heard across all of Moscow. The composer was incredibly matter of fact about this and never spoke of it again. To him it must have seemed as though he had entered a contract where he would produce specific works in return for the independence to write the pieces and compositions that he really wanted. But that is just when the screw turned.

6

Happiness and War

There must be many who welcome in the works of this Russian Playboy the absence of that oppressive pseudo-intellectuality and fatiguing emotionalism which are the bane of so much contemporary music. Prokofiev has kept a smile on his lips while others are grimacing, and for this alone we owe him a debt of gratitude.

Rollo H. Myers[1]

The year 1939 was important for Prokofiev's personal life. That summer, rather than going to his dacha in Nikolina Gora, the composer returned alone to holiday and work in Kislovodsk, a place close to his heart and directly linked with his younger pre-revolutionary days. It was here that, by all accounts, Prokofiev met the young woman who would soon become an indispensable part of his life – Maria Cecilia Abramovna-Mendelson, known commonly by the shorter name Mira Mendelson. When Prokofiev first met her, Mira was a student at the Gorky Literature Institute and an aspiring author. She was an only child, and her father was an economist who was well respected in the Communist Party. In accounts and memoirs that Mira kept diligently from her early days of meeting with Prokofiev, she does not dwell on the personal, preferring to focus on Prokofiev the great composer and expressing herself only as his humble assistant and occasional collaborator. Mira, completely in awe of this colossal artist, was in almost all respects the exact opposite of Lina Prokofiev. At this point Prokofiev and Lina were still married but living largely separate lives, communicating mainly through letter correspondence.

Sergei Prokofiev with Mira Mendelson, *c.* 1940s.

Mira tended to guard Prokofiev's artistic needs first and foremost. She was, variously, his administrator and archivist, creating the space and environments he needed to pursue his important work. She negotiated with bureaucrats on his behalf, and attended meetings when he was unwell or unable to attend. She appeared to have no significant people in her life apart from him and her parents. This meant that she was able to give the composer the attention that he needed. It was a challenging and unusual time in his career and Prokofiev would gradually come to rely on Mira a great deal. No doubt, having been raised within the Soviet Union and being the daughter of a respected party member, Mira was more adept at negotiating the niceties and complexities of the Soviet system, and she tirelessly helped the composer negotiate murky waters. Mira was very familiar with Prokofiev's new Soviet reality. She was also trained as a writer and was familiar with contemporary Soviet writers and sources, as well as knowing which sources might be looked upon more favourably than others. In all these respects, she was perfectly suited to take on the role of partner in his life, at a time when the composer's relationship with Lina was deteriorating fast. From their first meeting, they immediately started to discuss possible sources for operas and songs as well as ballet scenarios. Both shared a love for literature and the written word. Prokofiev respected this and Mira was the only collaborator the composer ever permitted to work on his opera librettos. The first work that was presented in public as a result of their collaboration was the cycle *Seven Songs*, op. 79, a set of tcxts that was in a strongly patriotic vein. Mira had supplied the verse for the fifth song. More broadly, however, her contribution to the composer's creative output remains misunderstood to this day.

Mira was completely loyal to Prokofiev and the mainstay of his life in the Soviet Union. Her artistic contribution to the composer's work as literary and critical support was incredibly important because she was part of the artistic process from the start. She worked on drafts, preparing the research on several projects such as *War and Peace*. She wrote unproblematic lyrics for his mass songs and picked out sources for his materials, like the *Winter Bonfire*. In his later years, she was a go-between for *The Tale of the Stone Flower*, taking opinions back and forth to the composer from the cultural bureaucrats when he was unwell. Twelve years of her life were unselfishly dedicated to Prokofiev; she cared for him until his death.

Given his personal (and soon enough professional) circumstances, Prokofiev must have found it difficult to keep a smile on his face. But despite so many challenges, he was personally happy; he had perhaps found affection and love again following his estrangement from Lina, but most importantly he was composing consistently without being constantly on the move. After so many years of international travel this was a welcome rest and brought him renewed focus on his work. He now had recognition for his compositions, winning six Stalin prizes between 1943 and 1951. He was proud of these awards, not least because they sustained the illusion that all continued to be well and that, in the eyes of his peers, he was a success. Internationally, his piano concertos continued to be performed frequently, along with the *Scythian Suite* and the Classical Symphony. Contemporary international journalism was less abrasive and critical – he was swiftly becoming a Russian classic and all tags of 'cleverness', Bolshevism and 'ugliness' had disappeared within a decade. His operas were hardly ever staged, however, and his symphonies were only occasionally heard, and so the West's perception of Prokofiev was one-sided at best. At home, he continued to work in all genres and to pursue his personal aesthetic goals.

During this happier period, the composer wrote some of his most powerful and beloved works for piano, the so-called 'War Sonatas'.[2] They are a triptych reflective of the times they were written in and characterized by his clear and uncompromising pianism. Prokofiev knew precisely what the art of performance entailed – stamina and physical strength, tempered with sensitivity to the larger forms underpinning each of these beautifully crafted sonatas. Physical athleticism, an unrelenting sense of urgency and infallible rhythm were always important features of his writing for the instrument. In this triptych, pacing and narrative come into their own as compositional drivers. The sonatas are underpinned by an element of ruthlessness in the way some of the darker themes are presented and explored – here the composer's tactile and embodied knowledge of the piano serves him well. Contrastingly, exquisite, soaring and long-limbed melodies provide an opportunity for reflection for both performer and listener; the projection of melodic materials is paramount. The influence of Meyerhold's theatre is never far away – in the works' gestures; in the use of repeated, incisive figures; in the manipulation of layers and registers and their accompanying effects. There are playful and humorous moments that can be heard by the listener and felt by the pianist; the unexpected turn of musical phrase, the purposely twisted cadence, the impish delayed rhythm and unprepared accents are all features of this humorous mode.

Prokofiev continued to premiere his own works himself, even after his return to the Soviet Union. He premiered Piano Sonata No. 6 in Moscow in April 1940. Later, having heard Sviatoslav Richter play and knowing that his piano sonatas would be in good hands, the composer gladly relinquished the premiere of Piano Sonata No. 7, in 1943, to the renowned pianist. Emil Gilels, an equally formidable performer, premiered Sonata No. 8 in 1944. At last Prokofiev felt he could focus his remaining energies on composing, while star Soviet artists premiered his works.

In March 1941 Prokofiev conducted Sviatoslav Richter in a performance of Piano Concerto No. 5. This would be Prokofiev's last performance in Moscow, and more poignantly, his last appearance in public with Lina by his side.

Meanwhile, the Second World War, designated by the Soviets as the Great Patriotic War, raged on, gradually and relentlessly closing in on the Soviet Union. By late spring Germany had occupied most of Europe while, as agreed in the Molotov–Ribbentrop pact, the USSR took possession of eastern Poland, as well as Lithuania, Latvia and Estonia. The Western world, as Prokofiev and Lina knew it, had been decimated. This must have been immeasurably painful to Lina because, isolated from Paris and Europe, not only would those Parisian years have seemed like a distant memory but her chances of returning to Europe were now non-existent. Further bureaucratic complications threatened her very existence. As Lina and Prokofiev had been married overseas, their marriage was not recognized by the Soviet authorities. The composer was therefore advised that he could marry his companion Mira at any time without needing a divorce. This was a terrifyingly ambiguous and tortuous situation for Lina who had given up her life, her modest career, her dreams and her material comforts to support Prokofiev's return to his homeland. Separating from Prokofiev would make her vulnerable and ultimately leave her with nothing. Eventually their marriage crumbled completely. In late March 1941 Prokofiev made the definitive move to leave his life with Lina behind, departing from the apartment on Zemlyanoy Val where he had lived with Lina, Sviatoslav and Oleg for a new life with Mira. Where Prokofiev saw an opportunity for a quieter life focused entirely on his art, Lina saw only uncertainty, deprivation and humiliation. The door had slammed well and truly shut on the woman who had stood by his side for almost two decades.[3] Despite this unorthodox and no doubt painful situation, Prokofiev, never lacking generosity with his loved ones, financially supported all of them even as he continued to develop his relationship with Mira.

Working hard on Prokofiev's behalf, Lev Atovmyan was in negotiations with the Soviet government for a new apartment for Prokofiev. By June 1944 Prokofiev finally had a two-room apartment on Mozhayskoye Shosse. Mira moved in with him in September 1944 and from that moment on, according to Lina's biographer Simon Morrison, Prokofiev 'no longer considered himself part of Lina's or his children's lives. He began to refer to Mira as his spouse, as did his colleagues – though all sides knew that she was not.'[4] His new apartment turned out to be very noisy and meant that, frustratingly for a composer intent on working systematically and to a routine, Prokofiev was forced to move again. His request for another apartment exchange was unsuccessful. The composer had no choice but to move in with Mira and her parents in an apartment where they had their own room. Though hardly the life of comfort he had been used to previously in the West, or even in his first years in the USSR, this was a luxury considering the situation

Sergei Prokofiev, with his sons Sviatoslav (centre) and Oleg, at the dacha in Nikolina Gora, *c*. 1950.

of their neighbours. Although it made for a cramped situation, the apartment was conveniently situated for Prokofiev: it was within walking distance of the Bolshoi Theatre, the Composers' Union and the conservatory. Prokofiev got on well with Mira's parents, who approved of her relationship with the composer. Indeed, when Mira's mother died during the war, the couple continued to live with

Sergei Prokofiev at the dacha in Nikolina Gora, *c.* 1950.

her father. Mindful of the situation he had created for Lina, even if he would not commit himself in public, Prokofiev continued to look for ways and to ask for help (from friends such as Atovmyan) to help expatriate Lina, who was now in an incredibly vulnerable position as she was no longer living with Prokofiev.

Amid such turbulence and incessant mental stress, it is perhaps unsurprising that Prokofiev might turn his attention to the world of fairy tales for his next project, *Cinderella*. But quiet domestic bliss was not to be, because the war intruded brutally.[5] *Cinderella* was replaced by the opera *War and Peace*, which Prokofiev had long wanted to write. Its time had come. His much longed-for tranquillity and quiet focus on composition disappeared as the Soviet Union, hideously unprepared for the attack of German forces, suffered some of the most gruesome experiences of the First World War, a war in which the Soviet people struggled against Nazi invasion. Leningrad was under siege for three years, and in December 1941 German units would approach within about 30 kilometres (20 mi.) of Moscow. With the Germans very close to taking over the city, the All-Union Committee on Arts Affairs evacuated leading artists from Moscow to Nalchik in the Caucasus. In August 1941 the composer and Mira joined others, like Nikolai Myaskovsky and Pavel Lamm, on a special train. Prokofiev left Lina, Sviatoslav and Oleg behind; they lived in the Chkalov apartment throughout the war. The trip to Nalchik took three days. During his evacuation period in Nalchik, Prokofiev appeared to have achieved a measure of contentment that had eluded him for several years, and certainly since he had been in the Soviet Union. Old friends noticed that

despite the depressed mood of those who surrounded him . . . He was happy, and this happiness was written on his face: it was always beaming. He was composing a great deal and with enormous inspiration, and, like all happy people, was filled with a sort of amazingly affectionate and kind attitude towards all those around him, with robust optimism . . . When they [Mira and Sergei] wandered, hand-in-hand, through the Nalchik marketplace in search of tomatoes or something else to eat, they were so busy with each other that they didn't notice anything or anybody.[6]

This period coincided, perhaps ironically, with a time of great productivity for Prokofiev. In fact, we might consider that the war years saw the creation of some of the composer's most colossal, influential and beautiful works, compositions that remain in the repertoire today. Between 1941 and 1944 Prokofiev completed the first version of his beloved opera *War and Peace*, Symphony No. 5, a string quartet, two piano sonatas, a flute sonata (which was also transcribed for violin), the ballet *Cinderella* and five film scores, among other works.

In Nalchik, Prokofiev concentrated on developing his ideas for *War and Peace*, a project that was dear to him and that had been on his mind for some time. Possibly spurred on by his newfound stability and contentment in his relationship with Mira, he worked together with her on researching the historical context, thinking through scenarios and working through all the sources. When Prokofiev came to bring to life his vision for *War and Peace*, he was not only an experienced operatic composer with a good understanding of what would work on the operatic stage, but was now a composer with several years' experience of working within the Soviet scene. This opera, at least as he saw it, was his magnum opus. He sensed, and perhaps hoped, that making an opera out of Leo Tolstoy's *War and Peace* would be his greatest achievement, the enactment and culmination of his operatic manifesto as he conceived it. Prokofiev did not intend a literal interpretation or simply a representation of the source novel, which would be impossible anyway, but rather the re-envisioning and re-enactment of the book for a Soviet-cultured audience and beyond.

Prokofiev initially wanted to call his great project *Natasha Rostova: Scenes from My Life*. In the composer's ideal world, Tolstoy's novel not only had intrinsic operatic potential in many of its powerful and emotional scenes but would enable him to represent different planes of action: to juxtapose, for example, the epic battle and war scenes with the domestic, a contrast that always interested him. Tolstoy's text gave the composer plenty of opportunity for exploring and developing characterization, with the full forces of a Soviet orchestra and a Soviet theatre at his disposal. This was the composer's ideal vision for *Natasha Rostova/War and Peace*. Unhappily, driven by well-honed cultural bureaucratic processes, the final version turned out to be a very different proposition.[7]

Prokofiev returned from Nalchik to Moscow in the winter of 1942 with *War and Peace* on his mind. The plan was for him to work with Samuil Samosud, a conductor at the Bolshoi Theatre, on a possible production. Samosud arranged a hearing for the staff of the Bolshoi in mid-January 1943. Although Samosud remained an ardent supporter of the opera, wartime conditions meant that the creation of a working schedule, while so many artists were dispersed all over the Soviet Union, would be an impossible task. The premiere would need to be delayed. Prokofiev and Mira were then moved to Tbilisi, where they stayed for about six months in a hotel near Yerevan Square. During this period Prokofiev seized the opportunity to immerse himself in the theatre that he loved so much. He saw works by Shakespeare, Balzac and Sheridan, attended symphonic concerts and watched European and Georgian operas. He also continued to work with Mira on the war scenes of *War and Peace* and managed to perform in public quite a few times while in the Georgian city.

From Tbilisi the couple moved yet again, to Alma-Ata (present-day Almaty) in Kazakhstan, where the Soviet film director and theorist Sergei Eisenstein was working in the Soviet film studios. Their journey took them across the Caspian Sea and by train across the desert. Despite the shortages that they faced in Alma-Ata, including of food and water, Prokofiev and Mira had a much more stable life in comparison to the gruesome chaos and starvation that cities like Leningrad (under siege for nearly a year by this time) were undergoing. Wartime correspondence between Prokofiev and Myaskovsky demonstrates the composer's commitment to his art and his relief at having a period of relative focus. He was working on several compositions simultaneously. Whether he had time to think beyond that and contemplate the political situation is anyone's guess. But Prokofiev's tendency to immerse himself in his work, sometimes to the exclusion of all around him, even loved ones, suggests that at this point he was still secure in his own worth and standing. If Prokofiev had left the West with a view – idealistic and somewhat impossible as it might seem to us with hindsight – to return to the level of productivity to which his energy aspired, this was the period in which he achieved single-minded and undisturbed focus. It is perhaps surprising that he was able to write these works with such alacrity during a period of great material deprivation, but it is also true that limitations inspire creativity. The war itself, which had turned officialdom's focus away from the cultural sector, meant there was some freedom for composers to work uninterruptedly and unhindered. However, this lull was not to last, as Prokofiev would soon find out.

During the war years, the composer was, like so many others, in great financial need. Performances and commissions dried up. The faithful Atovmyan did his best to ensure that Prokofiev was materially provided for, ensuring that the expenses for his accommodation during the evacuation were covered. At that time Atovmyan was the director of Muzfond, a publishing house set up in 1939 and connected with the Union of Soviet Composers, and had even set up a small press that would pay composers for their work. He supplied Prokofiev with basic materials, such as manuscript paper, that he knew the composer would need. He also organized copies of piano reductions of the composer's works, arranged for their staging and took care of the finances that related to the composer's permanent separation from Lina. Prokofiev was also still trying to find a way to send Lina back to Paris and tried to enlist Atovmyan's help in this endeavour. Even though the couple were estranged, Prokofiev was very worried about Lina and his two sons, knowing that they were struggling even with basic necessities such as food. It was Atovmyan who organized vouchers enabling Lina and the boys to eat at the cafeteria of the Composers' Union in Moscow.

The summer of 1944 was spent in the Composers' Union residence in Ivanovo with other composers, including Shostakovich, his old teacher Glière, Aram Khachaturian and Yuri Shaporin. On their return to Moscow in autumn 1944, Prokofiev and Mira moved into a small apartment located near what is now Kutuzovsky Prospekt. Here they celebrated the start of what they hoped would be a year of release from the personal suffering and deprivation of wartime. In January 1945 Prokofiev conducted the premiere of Symphony No. 5, a symbolic event that was, in hindsight, to mark a slow but steady downward turn in his fortunes in his homeland. The composer had not embarked on this large-scale form for over fifteen years and this symphony was billed to a highly charged audience as the first Soviet symphony. Keen with anticipation, the bright lights of artistic Moscow took their seats in the Great Hall of the Moscow Conservatory. In a moment that would be prophetic for the last eight years of Prokofiev's life, Soviet cannons, celebrating the Red Army's march into Germany, suddenly exploded. Prokofiev stood calmly on the podium, waiting for the cannons to stop. Only then did the first performance of Symphony No. 5 commence. It crystallized the essence of an era for Soviet citizens with its heroic and epic tone. This symphony is completely unlike its predecessors, Symphonies Nos 3 and 4, which were linked to his opera *Fiery Angel* and the ballet *Prodigal Son* respectively and from which Prokofiev drew much of the musical materials. With Symphony No. 5, and certainly later with No. 6, the composer wrote non-programmatic works driven by entirely new melodic material characterized by tight structures, clear textures and his distinctive orchestral palette. The composer had time and consideration to lavish on each of his last three symphonies, and each one possesses their very own, yet peculiarly distinctive, Prokofievan personality.

But the years of deprivation, guilt and unrelenting compromise took their gradual physical as well as emotional toll on Prokofiev, who had always suffered from a number of ailments. Following his triumphant podium event, he suffered a fall at his Moscow apartment, resulting in a concussion. It would appear that his fall was caused by a spell of dizziness due to hypertension. This head injury marked a significant downturn in his health, and the last years of his life were marred by illness. It is unsurprising that the composer was suffering given the personal and professional scrutiny and pressure he constantly found himself under. Other figures in the public eye endured poor physical and mental health: his good friend and collaborator Sergei Eisenstein had suffered a heart attack the previous year. After his serious fall, Prokofiev was hospitalized and languished for a long period of time. Mira and his friends were deeply worried about how gravely ill he was, fearing the worst would now come. Mira was with him constantly, tending to his every need and attempting to buoy his spirits. Finally, as his health improved somewhat, he joined Eisenstein at a sanatorium in Barvikha, just outside the Moscow ring road and the city. He remained there for the spring as he convalesced. Doctors refused to allow him to compose but he found a way around that stricture by composing in his head, creating the outlines and ideas for *Ode to the End of the War*.

While Prokofiev was slowly convalescing, the premiere of his ballet *Cinderella*, which he wrote with Galina Ulanova in mind for the title role, was being prepared for an autumn performance. This took place on 21 November at the Bolshoi Theatre. It was an immediate success. The ballet was also staged in Leningrad the following spring and it remained in the repertoire of both the Kirov and the Bolshoi theatres. At the same time, rehearsals were taking place for the upcoming concert performance of *War and Peace*, which would be conducted by Samosud in June. Prokofiev spent the summer of 1945 at the Composers' Union resort in Ivanovo, preferring to be out in the countryside, where nature helped him focus. He would walk around the woods with a little notebook to capture themes and musical ideas, shapes and rhythms as they occurred to him. If he didn't have a notebook, he would use any scrap of paper or cigarette packet that he could find to record these themes. While his health continued to be fragile, mentally Prokofiev was still completely committed to creating new works. It was in this intellectual and physical space that the composer began conceptualizing Symphony No. 6.

Prokofiev completed work on this symphony in early 1947, as evidenced by the sketches and scores available to us. It was premiered by the Leningrad Philharmonic Orchestra, conducted by Yevgeny Mravinsky, on 11 October 1947. It is one of the most profound and powerful works that the composer wrote in these late years, showing a confident composer, master of his orchestral craft, uncompromising with his language and true to his distinctive sound. The skill is evident from the opening ten bars; Prokofiev is at the height of his command of forces, drama and atmosphere. Silences are paced with surgical precision; the dialogue across extreme textures and timbres (such as woodwinds versus brass) can be clearly heard. Compelling rhythmic motifs are contrasted with ethereal melodic lines.

Meanwhile, on their return to Moscow, Prokofiev and Mira joined her father in the apartment located on Moscow Art Theatre Lane. By autumn 1945, with the end of the war, a spirit of optimism pervaded not just the Soviet Union but the world more generally. Thoughts of rapprochement with Soviet musicians now seemed more possible. Prokofiev received letters from old acquaintances like Ephraim Gottlieb and Dukelsky as well as Serge Koussevitzky, who continued to champion his music in the United States and beyond. But his health would never be the same and Mira worked hard to ensure he was not placed under undue or unmanageable pressure. He was unable, for example, to travel to Leningrad for the premiere of his opera *Betrothal in a Monastery*, which took place at the Kirov Theatre on 3 November 1946.

But, as always with Prokofiev, life's blows did not break his spirit, at least not while he was still in adequate health. Life with Mira was routine and had little drama, which was of enormous benefit to him at this time. With a measure of optimism, and not knowing the chaos that was about to be unleashed, Prokofiev enlisted the help of Atovmyan to purchase a small dacha in Nikolina Gora. It was a simple and rustic cottage with basic amenities, where Prokofiev could focus on his composition undisturbed and where life was quiet and slow. This brought him great happiness. But even there, the tentacles of cultural policy would torment his final years.

7

The Year 1948 and Its Consequences

Who shall be loved? Who can be trusted?
With whom do we risk no betrayal?
Who weighs our words and deeds, adjusted
Obligingly to our own scale?
Who never blackens us with slander?
Who's there to coddle us and pander?
Who sees our sins as 'not too bad'?
Who will not bore us, drive us mad?
Stop your vain search for lost illusions:
You're wasting all your strength and health.
Alexander Pushkin[1]

If artists had hoped that the relaxation of state control over cultural policy would last, indications otherwise were evident as early as February 1946. Andrei Zhdanov, Stalin's cultural henchman, turned his focus to tightening cultural policy, starting first with a resolution on literature from the Central Committee of the Communist Party. This was followed by one on theatre and another on film, hailing the beginning of what became known as the Zhdanovshchina. Literary figures like the poet Anna Akhmatova and the satirist Mikhail Zoshchenko came under severe criticism. Part two of Eisenstein's *Ivan the Terrible* faced scrutiny because it demonstrated his 'ignorance of historical facts by showing the progressive bodyguards of Ivan the Terrible – the *oprichniki* – as a degenerate band'. The film was branded as 'formalist', which meant that the work was anti-populist in Soviet terms and deemed unacceptable for public consumption; Eisenstein was forced to publish an apology. At this point the attack on the film did not extend towards Prokofiev's score.

Musicians and composers were spared in this first wave of salvos, just as they had been a decade previously. Away from Moscow, Prokofiev was not as aware of these developments and their consequences as he might otherwise have been. In many ways he was able to hold on to the deep-seated optimism that had sustained him throughout the peaks and troughs of his entire career. He had spent the busy summer of 1947 in Nikolina Gora. As well as a revision of Symphony No. 4, Piano Sonata No. 9 and a sonata for solo violin, Prokofiev also wrote some requisite political works celebrating the thirtieth anniversary of the Bolshevik Revolution. These included the festive poem *30 Years*, op. 113, for symphony orchestra, as well as a cantata for mixed chorus and orchestra entitled *Flourish, Oh Mighty Land*, op. 114. He pursued further work on the revisions to his opera *War and Peace*, as well as on Symphony No. 6. Mira continued to act as his assistant–secretary–nurse as necessary, ensuring that any energy that Prokofiev still had was focused entirely on composition.

January and February 1948 were significant for Prokofiev both personally and professionally. He married Mira on 13 January in a civil ceremony in the Sverdlovsk district. They celebrated their nuptials quietly. Prokofiev had been living with Mira for the past seven years; we can only speculate why the composer chose this moment to officially marry her. Neither Mira nor Prokofiev make any mention of this event in their memoirs or personal writings, so conjecture is all we are left with. Some scholars have even suggested that there might have been a sinister explanation for this, whereby party officials might have encouraged Prokofiev to marry Mira to ensure that his first wife, Lina, was as removed from the composer as possible as she was vulnerable to being picked up by the secret police. But this, too, is just guesswork.

In early 1948 the ostensibly innocuous opera *The Great Friendship* by the Georgian composer Vano Muradeli came under heavy criticism. In chilling echoes of the 1936 Shostakovich debacle, the

Yevgeny Mravinsky and Sergei Prokofiev at the premiere of the latter's Symphony No. 6, 1947.

attack on music from above commenced with one specific work and then grew to include almost every Soviet composer, including the top five: Prokofiev, Shostakovich, Khachaturian, Myaskovsky and Kabalevsky. This swiftly turned into a vicious attack during which none of the established Soviet composers were spared. The attacks snowballed. They were bitter and unrelenting, and in this nightmarish environment, as Shostakovich put it, 'everyone seemed to go mad.'[2] Composer critiqued composer, whether they wanted to or not. Prokofiev was not spared and those minor composers who had for long held a grudge against this foreign and 'French' composer, as they sometimes called him behind his back, took advantage of the moment and piled on. Pettiness, small-mindedness and even cruelty were permissible and even encouraged.

In mid-January 1948 Moscow composers were summoned to a three-day plenary meeting, ostensibly designed to find ways of eliminating the dreaded element of Formalism from Soviet music. During this conference, which Prokofiev was not able to attend, figures like the composer Victor Bely and the principal of the Leningrad Conservatory took the opportunity to vehemently critique the opera *War and Peace*. In a desperate attempt to prevent their own denunciation, composers turned on one another. Those who came under criticism in this three-day plenary suddenly found themselves persona non grata. Prokofiev's public humiliation was now complete. The composer never fully recovered from what he saw as a terrible betrayal by those he considered colleagues and close acquaintances. He also could not comprehend the mindset behind such meaningless and untruthful accusations. But the die was cast with no resolution in sight.

Prokofiev's music, which for quite some time now had been heard and programmed frequently in the big halls across the Soviet Union, and especially in the cities of Moscow and Leningrad, was no longer performed and was dropped from the repertoire. The private discussions were summarized in an official party resolution ('On the Opera *The Great Friendship* by Muradeli') that was made public and released by the party's Central Committee. It appeared publicly on 10 February 1948. Prokofiev, who was not able to attend these endless orgies of self-censoring, accusation and disparagement due to ill-health, was advised to write an apology that would be read out in his absence instead. In his response, he accepted the ruling of the party officials and expressed concerns over how the alien nature of Formalism could lead to a diminished musical understanding. Mustering all his energy, Prokofiev tried to remain focused on the future, describing the next opera he was working on, *Story of a Real Man*, which would deploy what he considered to be a clean-cut harmonic language with strong lyricism.

The professional betrayal was swiftly followed by a personal one. Even while the plenary conference was taking place, Prokofiev's sons informed him that their mother, Lina, had been taken away by the police, and agents with search warrants had arrived to ransack the apartment on Chkalova Street. Her arrest was on suspicion of being a spy. Using the pretext that a package needed to be picked up for a friend, Lina was lured out of the apartment to the nearest train station where she was forcefully picked up and taken to the Lubyanka prison. She was charged with the crime of passing information to foreigners, a common charge during this period. No evidence was ever found to corroborate it; in any case, she would not have had access to any classified information so it is reasonable to accept that the charge was fabricated. Her only crime was that she was fluent in several foreign languages, moved in diplomatic circles and had an international and cosmopolitan upbringing. In those times, this was more than sufficient for her to be incriminated as a foreign element. She was eventually released in 1956 as part of Nikita Khrushchev's campaign to make amends to the victims of the Stalinist purges. After Lina was forcefully abducted and carted off to the Gulag, it would be years before she saw her sons again, not being reunited until after Stalin's death. Although her foreign credentials and her conspicuous inability to fit into Soviet society might have contributed to her arrest, there was clearly nothing coincidental about it. It was synchronized with attacks on Prokofiev and others in 1948. The composer would never see Lina again.

After the fateful February 1948 trials of the Soviet music world, Prokofiev returned to his dacha, his place of safety in Nikolina Gora, to bury himself in work on his opera *The Story of a Real Man*. This opera was based on Boris Polevoi's novel with the same title. Despite his woes with the previous attempt at creating a Soviet opera, the composer continued to focus on making this work acceptable, permitting himself to simplify his ideas and idiom to a level he had never previously fathomed or found acceptable. In this work he was influenced by the tradition of the Soviet song opera, as well as by his own recent cantatas and oratorios. This was as far away from the principles of opera that he had held on to throughout his career as was possible for him to countenance. The emphasis on uncomplicated lyricism was tempered but never to the extent that it became wholly predictable. Prokofiev may have been physically unwell and artistically beleaguered, but he was not yet ready to fully concede defeat. He had worked with mass songs, and he knew very well that this opera would come under severe scrutiny.[3] Thus, he turned to a more pronounced use of a folk idiom, with a sustained use of closed forms and genres that had the ultimate (and non-Prokofievan) effect of breaking up his usual rhythmic and dramaturgical drive.[4]

The reception of *The Story of a Real Man* behind closed doors on 20 December 1948 was not a pleasant one. It was clear that the party had not yet finished punishing and humiliating Prokofiev. Cultural and musical bureaucrats sought to downplay, yet again, the composer's obvious efforts to reform his Formalist ways and criticized the performance and the work. Prokofiev was angry and humiliated by the appalling performance musicians from the Kirov Theatre produced for this occasion. Later that month, in a plenary session at the Union of Soviet Composers, the secretary of the union and a minor composer in his own right, Tikhon Khrennikov, seized the opportunity to further criticize *Real Man* in a most public and degrading way, arguing that Prokofiev had not learnt his lesson and Formalism still was evident in this work. The composer would never see the opera staged; all plans for a production were aborted.

At the time, it was also suggested to Prokofiev that he transform his two-night opera *War and Peace* into a single-evening presentation. Desperate to see one of his recent major works reach the stage, the composer made these revisions, which were many, resulting in a thirteen-scene version (one of several versions) of the opera. Given that the composer's work on *War and Peace* took place alongside his work on other musical projects during the period of the Second World War, it was a prime target for politicization. Hence, Prokofiev was repeatedly tasked with adding episodes that reflected the heroic nature of the people's war spirit, and to create an enhanced role for General Kutuzov, who, over multiple requested revisions to the music and insertion of the crowd scenes, became a symbol for Stalin within the opera. The composer disagreed with these changes for musical reasons especially – to his mind the opera that was initially conceptualized as 'scenes from a life' was forced to be writ large to reflect the inescapable tragedy of the war at the time and portray Stalin as a contemporary hero and saviour of the nation. But the ever-meticulous Prokofiev saw, in these changes, the theatrical rhythm of his work, designed and carefully structured, stretched to achieve an elasticity never intended. Ultimately he made those changes because he wanted his magnum opus, as he conceived of it, to be staged. Yet the alterations were simply not enough to satisfy a bureaucracy that had made clear the composer was to remain a major target for criticism.

These were crushing blows for the normally resilient and optimistic Prokofiev. After working on these operas for so long, only to see them ripped apart by Soviet bureaucrats who had no interest in supporting his work and who would rather see him disgraced, the composer was desperate. A sweet letter from his old friend Vera Alpers urged him not to despair despite the situation. Once again, we see him as a creature of habit; despite his circumstances, he turned once more to work, composing his seventh and final ballet, *The Tale of the Stone Flower*. In this ballet, the composer created his most discernibly Russian-sounding work. Here, the stylistic and compositional techniques that an audience, both contemporary and present, might associate with exoticism are immediately evident. These included the pentatonic scale, plagal cadences and melodic nuances that often play on a flattened submediant. The ostinato, ever an important compositional tool for Prokofiev, is deployed here too but has a very different structural function than it had in the earlier works like *Fiery Angel*. However, once more, Khrennikov – who had never forgiven Prokofiev for not awarding him the highest mark in his conservatory final exam in composition – would, in a hallmark act of petty vengeance of this period, make sure that neither the operas nor the last ballet would reach the stage: a bureaucrat of mediocre talents bringing a titan of twentieth-century music to his knees.

In hindsight, these final years were certainly an inhumane tragedy that might and could have been averted had the main players in the drama been different and had the contextual environment enabled it. The extreme reactions to *The Story of Real Man* made no logical sense to Prokofiev. He could not begin to understand what the bureaucrats found objectionable in a work that he had been so careful with. He continued, insisted even, on being rational about what the Union of Soviet Composers expected from his music, despite the context being irrational and chaotic, driven by self-interest and professional survival. Relying on reason did not provide him with any answers. His wife Mira describes

Sergei Prokofiev playing through some musical ideas from his famous sketchbooks to Mstislav Rostropovich, 1952.

how the composer digested the fateful events of 3 December: he paced frantically around the room mumbling over and over, 'I just don't get it!'[5] It is likely that the repercussions of this public denial would have been immediately evident to him, but the wilful misunderstanding of his music and the integrity of his intentions would have been much less comprehensible.

Despite this chaos and betrayal, he continued to produce music of unquestionable calibre as well as aesthetic truthfulness and integrity. His self-belief and indomitable nature, along with the ever present Mira, sustained him in this period, during which he produced Symphony No. 7, full of portent and pathos, as well as Piano Sonata No. 9. Impressed by the playing of the young cellist Mstislav Rostropovich, Prokofiev wrote his sonata for cello, op. 119. In the composer's hands the instrument reaches musical heights and a profoundness that resonated with the times it was written in, but also, one might imagine, with the composer's state of mind. The lyrical lines of the first movement are simultaneously evocative and terrifying. The ethereal suspended moments, born of Prokofiev's love of the *skazka* (fairy tale) are spellbinding, especially in the first movement where they interact with some sublime piano writing. Here lyrical elements of writing are turned on their heads, melodies are expanded and stretched beyond recognition. Indeed, in this work, if one wanted to be speculative about it, Prokofiev seems to have processed some of the violence that may have been on his mind, and the trauma he was personally undergoing.

Mindful as ever of a Soviet composer's duty to be useful to upcoming generations, a principle to which he had, in his own way, always ascribed, he turned his attention once more to writing for children and young people. He composed the *Ballad of an Unknown Child*, a cantata for soprano, tenor, chorus and symphony orchestra, as well as *Winter Bonfire*, op. 122 (1940–50), a children's suite for boys' choir and orchestra. Perhaps he considered that writing for children was an unobjectionable pursuit; in any case, both works were well-received.

In his usual economical approach, Prokofiev crafted several suites derived from *The Tale of the Stone Flower*. Wary that if the full ballet were not to be staged it would be yet another composition consigned to the unprofitable drawer, in 1951 he completed three orchestral suites: *Wedding Suite*, op. 126; *Gypsy Fantasy*, op. 127; and *Ural Rhapsody*, op. 128. *The Mistress of the Copper Mountain*, op. 129, was a planned orchestral suite that remained unrealized. In the couple of years before his death, Prokofiev grumbled but did as he was told, yet the criticism of his work by the authorities continued post-1948. He was asked to flesh out the orchestration of *The Tale of the Stone Flower* and to further dramatize the narrative. Even though the composer had lost none of his acerbic response – calling the request haunting and disgusting – he did what he was asked to do. He mocked the concert master of the Bolshoi Theatre, Semyon Stuchevsky, for visiting him twice a week to explain the square bars required for the Russian dance. Prokofiev was not immune to the disrespect inherent in this gesture.

The orders from above were not just for simplification but for making the music basic – almost as though the cultural apparatus wanted to control the work so much as to co-compose it with

Prokofiev. He realized that his compromise at the hand of the regime was now complete, but knew that he had not much choice and no real opportunity for comeback.

The final five years or so of Prokofiev's life are full of works that started with good intentions and – most importantly – lofty ideals, but that were reduced to a quiet hush as though the composer had neither the inclination nor the aesthetic compulsion to complete them. Of these works, quite unsurprisingly, two operas remain – *Khan Buzay* and *Distant Seas*. Both incomplete operas demonstrate Prokofiev's stubborn commitment to the operatic form, even though by that point it was much transformed and diluted from his original vision of the previous decade. Rather than creating a dramatic crescendo of narrative action and music, the composer wove the opera together in smaller sections, built around short structural set-pieces. This might be due to the effect of film composition on his writing, but the research and materials that Prokofiev considered using point to an interest in playing with smaller structural forms to enable a swift response to censorship, which he had now come to expect. The archival manuscripts available to us demonstrate the lengths that the composer would go to in order to achieve such a realistic sound. With *Khan Buzay*, Prokofiev was drawn to setting a mythical text and legend to music. He worked with Mira to conduct the research into the context surrounding the legends and together they prepared a libretto. Work started on this project in 1943 but progressed slowly; Prokofiev had to put it aside until 1946 as he needed to turn his attention to other compositions in the meantime.

Another opera that remains incomplete, and which is certainly worth a mention, is *Distant Seas*. The sketches that remain for this opera indicate that Prokofiev was working seriously on this project in the summer of 1948, preparing the harmonic skeleton and making notes on syllabification patterns for text-setting. *Distant Seas* was planned as a lyric comic opera based on the vaudeville by Ivan Dykhovichny. From the materials available to us, it is again clear that Prokofiev planned a sectional approach to the opera. Throughout the scenario the indications are that musical structure would be in sections with a focus on lyricism. Of the 39 bars that remain of the overture, we can see that it opens with an eight-bar melody for solo flute, possibly indicating the lyrical event of the work. It seems clear that Prokofiev was intent on continuing to write on his own terms until the end. Whether the works were left incomplete because he ran out of time or because he had other pressing compositional priorities is hard to say. In these works, we can nonetheless see the essence of a composer whose main love remained the operatic stage, and his unrelenting focus on this form. His perseverance, despite the lack of operatic success Prokofiev had in his lifetime, is nothing short of heartbreaking.

To his last days, Prokofiev continued to pick his battles. His focus was on *War and Peace*, which he was determined to see staged. The pushback from his end towards any compositional advice or assistance was far greater when it came to this work – he had no intention of reducing it to the lowest common denominator. Although he was forced to make changes, such as the amplification of both the war and the waltz scenes, he was still comfortable that it was his hand that was writing this work, and that artistic, compositional and stylistic decisions remained his own. To stay focused and centred on his voice, despite the constant attack on musical individuality, he revisited works he had written earlier. He completed the revisions to the Symphony-Concerto (for cello) in 1952 then started a tenth piano sonata while also commencing a revision of Piano Sonata No. 5 from 1923. As though returning to an earlier confident and optimistic version of his artistic self in the days when he was aesthetically free, Prokofiev returned to his early works frequently, possibly seeking solace and self-confirmation as well as musical ideas.

Prokofiev chronicled his last year of life in an unpublished, personal diary.[6] Poignantly, it is starkly different to any of his earlier journals. Gone are the sparkly and witty vignettes of years prior, the tongue-in-cheek humour in its detailed description of every last thing that caught his eye. Instead, this final diary is heartbreakingly voiceless, as if the composer had lost the will to paint the world around him, to interact with it and to rationalize it. As the musicologist Natalia Savkina has argued, most of what

Sergei Prokofiev in front of the Miaskovsky plaque, c. 1951.

is included and referred to in this diary is 'determined by the invisible surveillance of external censorship'.[7] If Prokofiev was writing his previous diaries for posterity, this one is simply a factual account stripped of nuance, colour and personality. Indeed, Savkina has argued that the composer's readership of the last year of the diary was limited to the figures that he visited in private after Lina was arrested. It is impossible to know; certainly by this point, Prokofiev's entries had lost a great deal of the bravado and quick-witted energy that characterized the scribblings of the earlier years. Whether or not later and more sincere diaries pertaining to his Soviet experiences were written and destroyed immediately after his death is also difficult to ascertain. It is hard to understand how for an avid reflective writer like Prokofiev, personal documentation stops around 1936, and it is reasonable to imagine, or even hope, that he continued writing until much later in his life.

Personal and professional struggles followed the denunciations of 1948. His health would deteriorate gradually from this point onwards and it would be aggravated by the stress he sustained, the financial pressure, the gnawing self-blame behind Lina's arrest and her subsequent deportation to the camps.[8] These years were marked by doctor's visits, long medicine lists and trips to his beloved oasis of calm, Nikolina Gora. He may have been maligned by the state apparatus, but he was still loved and respected by many artists and even the occasional bureaucrat. His visitor list included the pianist Sviatoslav Richter and the cellist Mstislav Rostropovich as well as the conductors Samuil Samosud, Nikolai Golovanov and Yuri Fayer.

The last years of his life, like those of so many others in his situation at this time, including Shostakovich, would be lived in a kind of slow-motion torment – he could only survive his everyday reality if he continued to make time for creative work. This now came at a high physical and mental cost, and it soon became clear to those around him that he was no longer able to create with the intensity he was used to. But true to his indomitable spirit, even when the strain became too much and the doctors recommended a different regimen, he continued to find innocuous ways of sustaining his creative flow and process – whether through composing entire scores in his head or by notating key themes and ideas on napkins or whatever he had to hand (he was not permitted paper, for fear that composing would aggravate his situation).

In an unhappy and indeed tragic twist of fate, Prokofiev died on 5 March 1953, on the same day as Stalin. His funeral was ironically the sincerest event since his return to his beloved homeland. Only those who were closest to him, those who truly wanted to be there, made it to his burial.[9] The rest of the country was focused on participating in numerous funeral rites dedicated to the dictator under whose regime the artist, along with innumerable others, had suffered so much.

Time and again, when Prokofiev faced difficulties in life, whether personal or professional, music and the act of creation helped him cope and adjust. At this point in his life, when his originality, aesthetics and artistry became a matter of public debate by figures he considered, quite rightly, far from competent to be passing judgement, holding on to his creative instinct almost became a moral question. How he managed to create works of such beauty and mastery is testament to the uniqueness and strength of his prodigious, musical gifts.

In the final analysis, Prokofiev had been forced to realize that censorship and criticism from the top were the natural order of things in the state he lived in. He put up a good fight for several years and sought to mentally isolate himself from the insufficiencies and cruelties of Soviet society. In many ways the composer had come full circle, from being a complete iconoclast and innovator, to being compared to Tchaikovsky (intended as a compliment) in some late reviews of his work. Prokofiev must have been relieved that aspects of his late compositions were being compared with Tchaikovsky; he considered that to be a conduct of safe passage in his final years. And, in a strange twist of fate, that comparison prefigured his role in the twentieth century as one of the greatest classical composers of all time. These sad but nonetheless determined final years of his life demonstrated how his commitment to his art enabled him to transcend a material world so mercilessly focused on his destruction. It was only after his death that Prokofiev was ascribed his canonic status as an international giant of twentieth-century music – a status that scholars from either side of the East–West divide, for very different reasons, would only reluctantly bestow on him in the following decades. Today no doubts remain in the minds, hearts and ears of twenty-first-century audiences as to his place in our music histories. His music is everywhere – powerful, aspirational, awe-inspiring – and remains an example to this day that music and art can and will transcend the petty minds, deeds and horrors that relentlessly plague humanity.

References

Introduction: Prokofiev and Russia

1 From 'Scythians', a poem by Konstantin Balmont written (in Russian)
    in 1904, my translation.
2 In a strongly worded letter to Vladimir Nikolaevich Zederbaum sent
    from Ettal, 17 September 1923, he argues for the performance of his
    composition *Seven, They Are Seven*, completed several years earlier as
    an exemplar of his latest innovation in Russian music: 'I believe it is
    extremely important, for me and perhaps for Russian music, that it be
    performed as soon as possible.' Unpublished correspondence between
    the composer and Serge Koussevitzky's then-secretary, Zederbaum,
    Box 50, Folder 11, Serge Koussevitzky archive, Library of Congress
    Music Division, my translation.
3 Elena Dubinets, *Russian Composers Abroad: How They Left, Stayed,
    Returned* (Bloomington, IN, 2021), p. 7.
4 Much excellent scholarship exists on nationhood and nationality in
    Russian music. See, among others, Marina Frolova-Walker, *Russian
    Music and Nationalism from Glinka to Stalin* (New Haven, CT, 2007).
    Of broader scope is *National Identity in Russian Culture*, ed. Simon
    Franklin and Emma Widdis (Cambridge, 2004). I define Prokofiev's
    self-perception as Russian in the following paragraphs and continue
    to critique his often malleable identity throughout the present text.
5 'I receive letters from Russia, and I've also received a very interesting
    book by Asafyev titled "Symphonic Studies: On Russian Opera."
    Myaskovsky, Belyayev, and Lamm are at the helm of the State
    Publishing House . . . Yavorsky is leading Russian music education
    and is inviting Suvchinsky to join him.' Unpublished letter to Natalia
    Koussevitzky, dated 31 July 1922, Box 50, Folder 10, Serge Koussevitzky
    archive, Library of Congress Music Division.

6   I explore the evolution and deployment of these concepts throughout
    all of Prokofiev's operatic output in *The Operas of Sergei Prokofiev* (New
    York and Suffolk, 2020). The soviet operas are the subject of a full-
    length study by Nathan Seinen, *Prokofiev's Soviet Operas* (Cambridge
    and New York, 2019).

7   In the present text, it should be noted that Said's definition of the
    term 'exile' is used, and as he suggests it also carries with it 'a touch
    of solitude and spirituality'. An émigré is 'anyone who emigrates to
    a new country. Choice in the matter is certainly a possibility.' See
    Edward Said, 'Reflections on Exile', in Said, *Reflections on Exile and
    Other Literary and Cultural Essays* [2001] (London, 2012), p. 181. In the
    case of composers like Rachmaninov, Stravinsky and so many others,
    one could easily argue that the political situation made it untenable
    for them to go back home thus forcefully making them into exiles.
    They were able to make sufficient and meaningful connection with
    their host countries and can be considered émigrés. Dubinets, *Russian
    Composers Abroad* explores and illuminates these complexities.

8   Sergey Prokofiev, *Diaries 1924–1933*, vol. III: *Prodigal Son*, trans.
    Anthony Phillips (London, 2012), entry 9 February 1929, p. 777.

9   Said, 'Reflections on Exile', p. 173.

10 To this day, there is very little theoretical scholarship on the music
    of Prokofiev largely because the composer did not inspire a school of
    composition, nor did he write in a contemporary avant-garde style
    such as twelve-tone writing.

11 Prokofiev clarifies his relationship with the venerable Russian teacher
    in an unpublished letter sent to British journalist Mr A. Fraser where
    he emphasized that he only studied orchestration with Rimsky-
    Korsakov. The lectures were structured in a way that one could
    get much from these classes, should one have the inclination and
    motivation or 'nothing at all' if one was indifferent. As he put it: ' I was
    then fifteen and sixteen years old and belonged to the second group. I
    learned to orchestrate only seven years later.' Dated 10 June 1929, Serge
    Prokofiev Archive, MS#1721, Correspondence Box 5, Series II.1.

12 Throughout this text I refer to modernism to mean a plethora of
    approaches to artistic work in the first half of the twentieth-century.
    Even though, as Carol Oja has elegantly explained, 'modernism has since
    become problematic for its imprecision,' my usage of the word in this
    text embraces the multiplicity of perspectives, ideas, style and innovation
    that characterized the exuberant chaos of the period. Carol J. Oja, *Making
    Music Modern: New York in the 1920s* (Kindle edn, 2000), location 88.

13 See, most recently, Rita McAllister and Christina Guillaumier, eds,
    Rethinking Prokofiev (New York, 2020).

14 Prokofiev continually negotiated his fees. For example, when he was
    invited to perform one of the piano concertos with the Nouveaux-
    Concerts du Theatre Cora-Laparcerie he was offered 500 francs,
    to which he responded, 'The fee you are offering is insufficient.'
    Unpublished letter dated 28 November 1923, Serge Prokofiev Archive,
    MS#1721, Correspondence Box 1, Series II.1 (in French, my translation).

15 Reference will be made to Prokofiev's ballet works throughout the
    present text. A full account of his early ballets can be found in Stephen
    D. Press, *Prokofiev's Ballets for Diaghilev* (New York and London, 2006).
    Detailed accounts of his later ballets may be found in Simon Morrison,
    The People's Artist: Prokofiev's Soviet Years (New York, 2008).

1 The Road to Petersburg

1 From an interview published in *The Musical Observer* by Frederick
   Martens, New York, 1918. Cited in Vladimir Blok, ed., *Sergei Prokofiev:
   Materials, Articles, Interviews* (Moscow, 1978), p. 27. The article was
   retranslated from Russian by Andrew Markow.

2 Sergei Prokofiev, *Prokofiev by Prokofiev: A Composer's Memoir*, ed. David
   H. Appel, trans. Guy Daniels (New York, 1979), p. 12.

3 Christina Guillaumier, 'A Genealogy of Prokofiev's Musical Gestures
   from the *Juvenilia* to the Later Piano Works', in *Rethinking Prokofiev*,
   ed. Rita McAllister and Christina Guillaumier (New York, 2020),
   pp. 299–316.

4 Prokofiev, *Prokofiev by Prokofiev*, p. 19.

5 Ibid., p. 35.

6 Pamela Davidson's translation of a literary notebook belonging to
   Prokofiev's mother is one of the resources available to researchers.
   It is dated 1917 and records various 'items of relevance to her son's
   creative work and reading'. See Pamela Davidson, '"Look After Your
   Son's Talents": The Literary Notebook of Mariya Prokofieva', in *Sergey
   Prokofiev and His World*, ed. Simon Morrison (Princeton, NJ, 2008),
   pp. 3–59.

7 Prokofiev remembers that his mother particularly liked playing
   volume I of Beethoven's piano sonatas.

8 Sergey Prokofiev, *Diaries 1907–1914*, vol. I: *Prodigious Youth*, trans.
   Anthony Phillips (London, 2006), p. 445.

9　Many of Prokofiev's operas are strongly rooted in the fantastic, particularly with the 'extravagant fancy' and 'eccentric' connotations of the term, rather than the moment of hesitation as described by Tzvetan Todorov in his seminal treatise on the fantastic. See Tzvetan Todorov, *Introduction à la littérature fantastique* (Paris, 1970); Todorov describes the fantastic as the moment of hesitation experienced by readers when they are faced with a situation that conflicts with their perception of reality. For an analytical evaluation of all of Prokofiev's operas, see Christina Guillaumier, *The Operas of Sergei Prokofiev* (New York and Suffolk, 2020).

10　David Nice, *Prokofiev: From Russia to the West, 1891–1935* (New Haven, CT, 2003), p. 15.

11　Ibid.

12　Prokofiev, *Prokofiev by Prokofiev*, p. 44.

13　Ibid., pp. 54–5.

14　For his entrance exam in obligatory piano, Prokofiev played scales, arpeggios, scales in thirds, a Bach fugue and a Beethoven sonata and was also given a sight-reading piece. At the end of the exam, Winkler's assessment was that 'You read music rather well, and you don't play badly, although you need more technique.' See ibid., p. 109.

15　For an excellent overview of the curriculum at the St Petersburg Conservatory at this time, see А. Н. Ахонен (A. N. Akhonen), *Прокофьев в Петербургской консерватории* [Prokofiev at the St Petersburg Conservatory], vol. XIV, St Petersburg Music Archives (St Petersburg, 2016).

16　In a letter to a journalist who was writing a piece about him, Prokofiev pointed out that 'at the Conservatoire I have been in constant opposition to its academicism, and the Russian nationalism did not interest me until 1915 when Diaghileff persuaded me to compose "Chout" in Russian style.' Unpublished letter to Mr A. Fraser, dated 10 June 1929, p. 2 of corrections, Serge Prokofiev Archive, MS#1721, Correspondence Box 5, Series II.1.

17　Nice, *Prokofiev*, p. 49.

18　Prokofiev describes Winkler in his memoir as 'untalented but extremely conscientious'. See Prokofiev, *Prokofiev by Prokofiev*, p. 150.

19　Ibid., p. 113. Two years earlier the young composer had been taught the simple rudiments of harmony by Glière and had consciously tried to discard this teaching, which he found far too academic.

20　Cited in Boris Berman, *Prokofiev's Piano Sonatas* (New Haven, CT, 2008), p. 35.

21 Prokofiev, *Diaries 1907–1914*, p. 47.

22 Ibid., p. 50.

23 Anna Nikolayevna Esipova (1851–1914) was a Russian pianist and renowned pedagogue who joined the teaching faculty of the St Petersburg Conservatory in 1893. She trained at the St Petersburg Conservatory under Theodor Leschetizky, whom she married in 1880. Her London debut came in 1874, followed by Paris in 1875 and the USA a year later. Anna Esipova was a legendary performer and an influential teacher who taught an entire generation of pianists. She was particularly famed for her singing tone and fine touch. Apart from Prokofiev, among her more famous students were Maria Yudina, Isabelle Vengerova, Leo Ornstein and Thomas de Hartmann. She was a popular teacher at the conservatory and her classes were large.

24 Prokofiev, *Diaries 1907–1914*, p. 71.

25 Sergey Prokofiev, *Diaries 1924–1933*, vol. III: *Prodigal Son*, trans. Anthony Phillips (London, 2012), p. 38; also, Sergey Prokofiev, *Diaries 1915–1923*, vol. II: *Behind the Mask*, trans. Anthony Phillips (London, 2008), pp. 532–3.

26 Prokofiev, *Diaries 1907–1914*, p. 124.

27 Ibid., p. 119.

28 Ibid., p. 118. When the composer brought Esipova his first piano sonata, she took it home with her and inserted detailed pedal markings.

29 Ibid., p. 129.

30 Ibid., p. 244.

31 Prokofiev mentions the repertoire he was working on at various points in his diaries.

32 Prokofiev, *Diaries 1907–1914*, p. 315.

33 Ibid., p. 553. *Legenda* is the sixth piece in op. 12, *Ten Pieces for Piano.*

34 Ibid., p. 319.

35 Ibid., p. 324.

36 Larry Sitsky notes that the Evenings of Contemporary Music was really the precursor to the Association of Contemporary Music (ACM) and came into existence in 1901. See *Music of the Repressed Russian Avant-Garde, 1900–1929* (Westport, CT, 1994), pp. 5–6. A full account of the Evenings of Contemporary Music is given in Patrick Zuk's illuminating critical biography of Myaskovsky; he translates it as 'Modern Music Evenings' (*Vechera sovremennoy muziki*). See Zuk's *Nikolay Myaskovsky: A Composer and His Times* (New York and Suffolk, 2021).

37 For further insight into the connection of Nouvel and Nurok with *Mir iskusstva*, see also Sjeng Scheijen, *Diaghilev: A Life*, trans. Jane Hedley-Prôle and S. J. Leinbach (London, 2009).

38 Richard Taruskin, *Stravinsky and the Russian Traditions: A Biography of the Works through Mavra*, vol. I (Berkeley, CA, 1996), p. 372.

39 Such influences are discussed at greater length in Suzanne Moisson-Franckhauser's *Serge Prokofiev et les courants esthéthiques de son temps* (Paris, 1974).

40 As Harlow Robinson has observed, Russian musical modernism 'is a contradictory phenomenon'. One might well argue, as he does, that it is a 'vague and spacious label' that has been stretched to include very different figures that include Scriabin, Stravinsky and Shostakovich alongside Prokofiev. See Harlow Robinson, *Sergei Prokofiev: A Biography* (Boston, MA, 1987), p. 469.

41 In his diary entry for the occasion, Prokofiev only mentions two of these pieces by name: *Fairy Tale* and *Snow*, the first composed in 1907 and later revised to form part of op. 3, the second composed in 1908.

42 Prokofiev, *Diaries 1907–1914*, p. 581.

43 Ibid., p. 67.

44 Op. 7 consists of two poems, *The White Swan* and *The Wave*.

45 Prokofiev, *Diaries 1907–1914*, p. 144.

46 See the facsimile edition of the 'Wooden Book', Sergey Prokofiev, *Dereviannaia kniga* (St Petersburg, 2009).

47 Sinfonietta for orchestra in five movements, op. 5, composed in 1909–14.

48 Prokofiev, *Diaries 1907–1914*, p. 189.

2 Coming of Age

1 Rollo H. Myers, 'Prokofiev and Twentieth-Century Music', *The Listener* (14 October 1936).

2 The ancient Scythians were a race of fighters on horseback. Aspects of Scythianism drove the development of Russian Futurist poetry, with which Prokofiev was intimately familiar. Vladimir Mayakovsky even wrote in the young Prokofiev's 'Wooden Book'. In her seminal post-Soviet article on the topic, E. Bobrinskaya demonstrates how Scythianism, while being important for shaping the avant-garde, was a complex force behind twentieth-century Russian art and culture (Ekaterina Bobrinskaya, 'Scythianism in Early Twentieth-Century Russian Culture and the Scythian Theme in Russian Futurism', *Art in*

Translation, VIII/2 (2016), pp. 137–68). The spirit of revolution sustains Scythian art; for a revolutionary generation of artists who were seeking a new expression, the primitive offered possibilities for new forms of expression. Russian culture of the period was connected to both Scythian mythology and the occult. The young Prokofiev was steeped in both. The composer's fascination with this topic is most obviously explored in his opera *Fiery Angel*. Beyond the scope of this text, but intriguing and complex nonetheless, is the connection of the Scythians with the 'White Race' in the late nineteenth- and twentieth-century racial myths, itself tied with the identification of Russia as a northern country.

3 For more on Scythianism as a concept in adjacent disciplines, see Michael Kunichika, *'Our Native Antiquity': Archeology and Aesthetics in the Culture of Russian Modernism* (Boston, MA, 2015) and Mark Bassin, Sergey Glebov and Marlene Laruelle, eds, *Between Europe and Asia: The Origins, Theories, and Legacies of Russian Eurasianism* (Pittsburgh, PA, 2015). Richard Taruskin contextualized the concept and its application to Russian music in Stravinsky and the Russian Traditions (Berkeley, CA, 1996).

4 Polina Dimova, 'The Sun-Sounding Scythian: Prokofiev's Musical Interpretations of Russian Silver Age Poetry', in *Rethinking Prokofiev*, ed. Rita McAllister and Christina Guillaumier (New York, 2020), p. 142.

5 Richard Taruskin, *Stravinsky and the Russian Traditions: A Biography of the Works through Mavra*, vol. I (Berkeley, CA, 1996), pp. 854–5, 951–66.

6 A recent account by Rupert Christiansen, *Diaghilev's Empire: How the Ballets Russes Enthralled the World* (London, 2022) provides insight into the impresario's world of ballet. Another excellent source on Diaghilev and his ballets is Sjeng Scheijen, *Diaghilev: A Life*, trans. Jane Hedley-Prôle and S. J. Leinbach (London, 2009).

7 Lesley Chamberlain, *Lenin's Private War: The Voyage of the Philosophy Steamer and the Exile of the Intelligentsia* (New York, 2006), p. 45.

8 Nicolas Nabokov, *Bagázh: Memoirs of a Russian Cosmopolitan* (New York, 1975), p. 72.

9 Dimova, 'Sun-Sounding Scythian', p. 144.

10 *Seven, They Are Seven* eventually received its premiere courtesy of the Russian émigré conductor and bass player Serge Koussevitzky in 1924, seven years after Prokofiev composed it. It was first performed in the Soviet Union in 1956, four years after the composer's death.

11 Sergey Prokofiev, *Diaries 1915–1923*, vol. II: *Behind the Mask*, trans. Anthony Phillips (London, 2008), p. 677.

12 Albert Coates (1882–1953) was an English conductor and composer. Born in St Petersburg, where his English father was a successful businessman,

he studied in Russia, England and Germany before beginning his career as a conductor in a series of German opera houses. He was a success in England conducting Wagner at the Royal Opera House, Covent Garden, in 1914, and in 1919 was appointed chief conductor of the London Symphony Orchestra. He was not able to secure a permanent conductorship in the UK after 1923 and for much of the rest of his life he guest-conducted in continental Europe and the USA. In his last years he took orchestral appointments in South Africa, where he died at 71.

13 Oleg Prokofiev, trans. and ed., *Sergei Prokofiev: Soviet Diary 1927 and Other Writings* (London, 1991), p. 253.

14 Prokofiev, *Diaries 1915–1923*, p. 76.

15 Vladimir Blok, ed., *Sergei Prokofiev: Materials, Articles, Interviews* (Moscow, 1978), p. 29.

16 18 March 1920, cited in Noelle Mann, 'And More on Prokofiev's Three Oranges!', *Three Oranges Journal* (November 1995), http://sprkfv.net.

17 Prokofiev, *Soviet Diary*, entry 10 February 1927.

3 Scythian on Tour: Early Travels and Beyond

1 Autograph from Adolph Bolm to Prokofiev in his 'Wooden Book', signed and dated New York, 24 September 1918. Bolm was a Russian-born American ballet dancer and choreographer who worked with the Ballets Russes in Paris. He also took part in their American tour before sustaining an injury, resulting in him having to stay on in the United States.

2 Sergey Prokofiev, *Diaries 1907–1914*, vol. I: *Prodigious Youth*, trans. Anthony Phillips (London, 2006), p. 454.

3 Ibid., p. 705.

4 Otto Kling, the director of the London branch of Breitkopf & Härtel (which acquired J. & W. Chester at the outbreak of the First World War), introduced Prokofiev to the composer Granville Bantock, principal of the Midland School of Music in Birmingham.

5 Prokofiev, *Diaries 1907–1914*, p. 708.

6 Ibid., p. 705.

7 Letter from Sergei Prokofiev to Nikolai Myaskovsky, dated 12 June 1914, in D. B. Kabalevsky, ed., *Perepiska: S S Prokof'ev i N Ia Myaskovskiy* (Moscow, 1977).

8 Letter from Sergei Prokofiev to Nikolai Myaskovsky, dated 10 April 1915, ibid.

9 Prokofiev left Petrograd for the Caucasus in September 1917. At the time, he imagined he would be leaving for a month, although his mother had made him pack all manner of luggage and boxes as they prepared their Petrograd apartment for rent.

10 Sergey Prokofiev, *Diaries 1915–1923*, vol. II: *Behind the Mask*, trans. Anthony Phillips (London, 2008), p. 241.

11 Ibid., p. 253.

12 Ibid., p. 292.

13 Fifteen years later the composer prepared a version for a chamber orchestra (op. 34a).

14 Prokofiev, *Diaries 1915–1923*, p. 87.

15 Ibid., p. 341.

16 Ibid., p. 332.

17 Unpublished letter to Mrs J Colbert, San Francisco, dated 16 January 1921, Serge Prokofiev Archive, MS#1721, Correspondence Box 1, Series II.1.

18 Prokofiev would be reunited with his mother two years later, in June 1920.

19 Prokofiev, *Diaries 1915–1923*, p. 405.

20 This is a constant source of frustration for Prokofiev. In a letter to Ernest Oeberg (the managing director of Koussevitzky's Russian Musical Editions and Gutheil Editions) dated 26 April 1923, the situation has not yet improved. Here he asks whether the suite he extracted from *Chout* should be engraved. 'For God's sake, expedite the work this summer, otherwise, by autumn, I will have six new major pieces ready: 1) the score of the Second Concerto, 2) its piano arrangement, 3) the score of the suite from "The Fiery Angel," 4) the piano arrangement of the same suite, 5) the score of the suite from "The Love for Three Oranges," 6) the Fifth Sonata for piano. When will all this see the light of day? And how can my music develop if three-quarters of it is not published?' Box 50, Folder 11, Serge Koussevitzky archive, Library of Congress Music Division (my translation).

21 In discussions with his agent Fitzhugh Haensel, Prokofiev makes clear the strength of the relationship between him and the Russian conductor, declaring that Koussevitzky is 'the best if not the only pull in the USA' and citing a Russian proverb that 'an old friend is better than two new ones.' Unpublished letter to Fitzhugh Haensel, dated 19 December 1928, Serge Prokofiev Archive, MS#1721, Correspondence Box 5, Series II.1.

22 Relations with Prokofiev's publishers were occasionally fraught, and he seems not to have always been aware of reprints of his work. This

was no doubt mostly due to his itinerant lifestyle during this period. In a letter to his publisher, Robert Foberg, he asks to have copies of the new op. 12 so that he can use the music in his upcoming concert tour of Western Europe (as he calls it). He also requests his five author's copies of op. 36. He was a stickler for all kinds of detail, both in his work and in his personal life. Unpublished letter dated 3 October 1923, Serge Prokofiev Archive, MS#1721, Correspondence Box 1, Series II.1.

23 Prokofiev, *Diaries 1915–1923*, p. 522. Maude Alice Burke was the American-born wife of Sir Bache Cunard. She had her own fortune in addition to that of her husband, which gave a certain amount of freedom to pursue her own interests. She became a glittering London-based hostess who also had a relationship with the British conductor and impresario Thomas Beecham. Coates would most likely have advised Prokofiev to ensure that Lady Cunard introduced his work to Beecham, who would have been able to open many doors for the young composer. Beecham had brought the Ballets Russes to London in 1911 and also supported the Russian baritone Feodor Chaliapine in Britain.

24 Ibid., p. 665.

25 Unpublished letter to Haensel, dated 11 January 1929, Serge Prokofiev Archive, MS#1721, Correspondence Box 5, Series II.1.

26 Prokofiev, *Diaries 1915–1923*, p. 340.

4 Transitional Years

1 Hans Christian Andersen, *The Fairy Tale of My Life: An Autobiography* [1847] (New York, 2000), p. 414.

2 Letter from Prokofiev to Natalia Koussevitzky, dated 8 July 1923, in *Selected Letters of Sergei Prokofiev*, ed. and trans. Harlow Robinson (Boston, MA, 1998), p. 179.

3 Sergey Prokofiev, *Diaries 1924–1933*, vol. III: *Prodigal Son*, trans. Anthony Phillips (London, 2012), entry 9 February 1929, p. 117.

4 Ibid., p. 696.

5 Nicolas Nabokov, *Bagázh: Memoirs of a Russian Cosmopolitan* (New York, 1975), p. 144.

6 Simon Karlinsky and Alfred Appel Jr, eds, *The Bitter Air of Exile: Russian Writers in the West, 1922–1972* (Berkeley, CA, 1977), p. 84.

7 Marlène Laruelle, *Russian Eurasianism: An Ideology of Empire*, trans. Mischa Gabowitsch (Washington, DC, 2008). Contemporary resurrections of Eurasianism should not be confused with the one

being described here. As Laruelle cautions, 'Neo-Eurasianism is too often equated with foreign policy discourse of the new Russian patriotic ideology. On the contrary, it must be grasped in its historical and philosophical context to take its rightful place in Russian intellectual history, whatever our judgement on it,' p. 13.

8 Prokofiev, *Diaries 1924–1933*, p. 21.

9 Prokofiev relinquished his Nansen passport in return for a special artist visa, which he refers to and translates in his correspondence with the Swiss Consulate as *sertificate de passage* [*sic*] (Serge Prokofiev Archive, MS#1721, Correspondence Box 5, Series II.1, 3 September 1928). This saga took quite some time to resolve. In his back-and-forth correspondence with the Swiss Consul in Lyon, Prokofiev took the opportunity to respond about the surprising modus operandi of this unusually lengthy paperwork process, which he viewed as an anomaly anathema to needs of a contemporary musician. Unpublished letter to the Swiss Consul in Lyon, dated 17 September 1928. Serge Prokofiev Archive, MS#1721, Correspondence Box 5, Series II.1.

10 For more on these new Soviet institutions, see Patrick Zuk, *Nikolai Myaskovsky: A Composer and His Times* (New York and Suffolk, 2021), especially Chapters Six, Seven and Eight.

11 The first edition of the correspondence between Prokofiev and Myaskovsky, which took longer than nineteen years to publish (from 1958 to 1977), is heavily redacted. Censored topics included the discussion of copyright for citizens of the Soviet Union, travel to and from the Soviet Union and so forth. In later correspondence from 1930, Myaskovsky also complains about specific shortages of goods in stores, for example. This kind of commentary is also redacted. Whether Prokofiev took the information shared with him with a pinch of salt since he had not experienced it directly during his visits to the USSR, or whether he attributed it to Myaskovsky's specific brand of melancholy, is impossible to tell. For a full and illuminating account of the uncensored correspondence, see Nelly Kravetz, ed., *С. С. Прокофьев и Н. Я. Мясковский. Переписка* [The Correspondence of Prokofiev and Myaskovsky] (Moscow, 2023).

12 The Persimfans ensemble (the name is an abbreviation of Pervïy Simfonicheskiy Ansambl'bez Dirizhyora (First Conductorless Symphonic Ensemble)) was an initiative of Lev Tsytlin, a professor of violin at the Moscow Conservatory. The orchestra gave its first concert in February 1922 and, despite it being an experimental ensemble, it had a successful existence for over a decade and championed the work

of living Russian composers. The music of Prokofiev and Stravinsky was frequently programmed.

13 Patrick Zuk, 'Prokofiev and the Development of Soviet Composition in the 1920s and 1930s', in *Rethinking Prokofiev*, ed. Rita McAllister and Christina Guillaumier (New York, 2020), pp. 19–37.

14 Prokofiev, *Diaries 1924–1933*, p. 6.

15 Ibid., p. 5.

16 Ibid.

17 Nabokov, *Bagázh*, p. 162.

18 Prokofiev, *Diaries 1924–1933*, p. 52.

19 Ibid., p. 779.

20 Ibid., p. 164.

21 Ibid., p. 299.

22 S. Shlifstein, ed., *Sergei Prokofiev: Autobiography, Articles, Reminiscences* (Moscow, 1959), p. 64.

23 Nonetheless a few years later Prokofiev continued to work on the publication of this work. His letters to his French publisher about the engraving of his symphony are full of dry humour. His sardonic style remains evident and, as ever, he does not mince words, calling out errors and demonstrating how things should be meticulously engraved. Unpublished letter dated 6 August 1928, Serge Prokofiev Archive, MS#1721, Correspondence Box 5, Series II.1.

24 See also Christina Guillaumier, 'Ambiguous Modernism: The Early Orchestral Works of Sergei Prokofiev', *Tempo*, LXV/256 (April 2011), pp. 25–37.

25 Les Six was a French group of composers comprised of Auric, Honegger, Milhaud, Poulenc, Durey and Tailleferre. The group was assigned the soubriquet by the critic Henri Collet in Comœdia (16 January 1920). The French poet and playwright Jean Cocteau enthusiastically promoted the group, often dogmatically opining that French music should be liberated from foreign, especially German, influences.

26 Prokofiev, *Diaries 1924–1933*, p. 299.

27 Vernon Duke, whose real name was Vladimir Dukelsky (1903–1969), was to become a close friend of Prokofiev and one of his genuine contacts in the West even after his return to the Soviet Union. Dukelsky was born in Kiev and raised in an aristocratic family. He studied at the Kiev Conservatory, where he was taught by Glière (Prokofiev's first music tutor) and was a contemporary of Vladimir Horowitz. The civil war that broke out after the Russian Revolution forced his family, like so many other refugees, including Prokofiev's mother, to flee to Constantinople

for sanctuary. He eventually settled in New York and became close with George Gershwin. He became one of the most renowned Tin Pan Alley composers and combined this with writing music for Diaghilev's Ballets Russes under his birth name. He was thus able to use an alter ego for popular songs, while keeping his original name for works in the Western art tradition. Prokofiev continued to observe his career wistfully, no doubt wondering whether he could have achieved some similar balance had he not decided to return to the USSR. Dukelsky remembers Prokofiev's last visit to America with affection and sadness in his *Passport to Paris* (Boston, MA, 1955); Prokofiev, *Diaries 1924–1933*, p. 163.

28 Lesley-Anne Sayers, 'Re-Discovering Diaghilev's "Pas d'Acier"', *Dance Research: The Journal of the Society for Dance Research*, XVIII/2 (2000), pp. 163–85.

29 Prokofiev, *Diaries 1924–1933*, p. 185.

30 'London Letter', *Aberdeen Press and Journal*, 5 July 1927.

31 Prokofiev, *Diaries 1924–1933*, p. 151.

32 Ibid., p. 170.

33 Ibid., p. 73.

34 Ibid.

35 Ibid., p. 138.

36 Ibid., p. 341.

37 Ibid., p. 699.

38 Sergey Prokofiev, *Diaries 1915–1923*, vol. II: *Behind the Mask*, trans. Anthony Phillips (London, 2008), p. 442.

39 Ibid., p. 446.

40 Three versions of Prokofiev's *Fiery Angel* exist: the first dates from 1920–23; the second version (1926–7) is the performing version; a projected but incomplete third version also exists, dating from 1930. For a more in-depth discussion see Christina Guillaumier, *The Operas of Sergei Prokofiev* (New York and Suffolk, 2020). See also Simon Morrison, *Russian Opera and the Symbolist Movement, California Studies in 20th-Century Music*, 2nd edn (Berkeley, CA, 2019), pp. 201–63.

41 On a London tour in 1927 for example, Prokofiev notes that 'on her mood depends the entire outlook for our stay in London.' Prokofiev, *Diaries 1924–1933*, p. 669.

42 Francis Maes, *A History of Russian Music: From Kamarinskaya to Babi Yar*, trans. Arnold Pomerans and Erica Pomerans (Berkeley, CA, 2006), p. 318.

43 Noteworthy productions of *The Gambler* include Staatskapelle Berlin, 2008 with Daniel Barenboim, and Covent Garden, 2010 with Antonio Pappano.

44 Prokofiev, *Diaries 1924–1933*, p. 182.
45 Letter from Prokofiev to Nikolai Myaskovsky, 4 August 1925, in *Selected Letters of Sergei Prokofiev*, ed. Robinson, p. 25.
46 Unpublished letter to Vladimir Nikolaevich Zederbaum, dated 3 March 1924, Box 50, Folder 12, Serge Koussevitzky archive, Library of Congress Music Division.
47 Prokofiev stayed in touch with his mother's side of the family, the Raevskys, even when he was overseas, and ensured that funds were regularly sent to them. On his return to the Soviet Union Prokofiev remained in contact. Sadly his cousin Alexander Raevsky (known familiarly as Shurik) died in a camp (in Kansk) in 1942.
48 Prokofiev, *Diaries 1924–1933*, p. 363.
49 Oleg Prokofiev, trans. and ed., *Sergei Prokofiev: Soviet Diary 1927 and Other Writings* (London, 1991).
50 Prokofiev, *Diaries 1924–1933*, p. 343.
51 Ibid., p. 307.
52 Prokofiev, *Diaries 1924–1933*, p. 742.
53 Prokofiev, *Soviet Diary,* p. 81.
54 Ibid., p. 15, 20 January 1927.
55 Understanding this was a momentous point in his life; Prokofiev kept a lively diary of his first Soviet trip. See Prokofiev, *Soviet Diary* for a vivid, first-hand account of the composer–pianist's initial impressions on the first visit to his homeland since his departure almost a decade previously.
56 Unpublished letter to Warren Klein, dated 1 January 1929, Serge Prokofiev Archive, MS #1721, Correspondence Box 5, Series II.1.
57 *Sheffield Daily Telegraph,* 2 July 1929.
58 Prokofiev, *Diaries 1924–1933*, p. 735.
59 'A New Ballet by Prokofiev', *The Times*, 2 July 1929.
60 Prokofiev, *Diaries 1924–1933*, 9 February 1930, p. 919.
61 Aram Khachaturian, 'A Few Thoughts about Prokofiev', in *Sergei Prokofiev,* ed. Shlifstein, p. 200.

5 The Search for a New Freedom

1 Anna Akhmatova, *Selected Poems*, trans. Walter Arndt (Woodstock and New York, 2003).
2 Prokofiev in S. Shlifstein, ed., *Sergei Prokofiev: Autobiography, Articles, Reminiscences* (Moscow, 1959), p. 82.

3   Katerina Clark, *Moscow, the Fourth Rome: Stalinism, Cosmopolitanism and the Evolution of Soviet Culture, 1931–1941* (Cambridge, MA, 2011), p. 15.

4   Kevin Bartig, *Composing for the Red Screen: Prokofiev and Soviet Film* (Oxford, 2013).

5   Cited in Nelly Kravetz, 'Sergei Prokofiev and Levon Atovmyan: The Story of a Unique Friendship', in *Rethinking Prokofiev*, ed. Rita McAllister and Christina Guillaumier (New York, 2020), p. 114.

6   Clark, *Moscow, the Fourth Rome*, p. 15.

7   Ibid., p. 12.

8   Ibid., p. 6.

9   Sergei Radlov was an experimental director who trained with Meyerhold between 1913 and 1917 before embarking on his own career. His enormously successful production of *The Love for Three Oranges* took place in Leningrad on 18 February 1926. Radlov also directed the operatic works of Franz Schreker, Alban Berg and Richard Strauss, being the first to bring an expressionist opera to the Soviet stage. For more on Radlov, see David Zolotnitsky, *Sergei Radlov: The Shakespearian Fate of a Soviet Director* [1995] (Oxford and New York, 2015).

10 Cited in Simon Morrison, *Lina and Serge: The Love and Wars of Lina Prokofiev* (Boston, MA, and New York, 2013), p. 183. See also the original memoirs by Alice Berezovsky, *Duet with Nicky* (Boston, MA, 1943).

11 Morrison, *Lina and Serge*, p. 184.

12 Cited in Simon Morrison, *The People's Artist: Prokofiev's Soviet Years* (New York, 2008), p. 43.

13 M. D. Calvocoressi, 'Prokofiev and Classicism', *The Listener* (10 May 1933).

14 Rollo H. Myers, 'Prokofiev and Twentieth-Century Music', *The Listener* (14 October 1936).

15 Georges Auric, 'A New Prokofiev Concerto', *The Listener* (16 December 1936).

16 Norman Suckling, 'Stravinsky and Prokofiev', *The Listener* (31 March 1937).

17 *Western Morning News*, 28 January 1938.

18 *Yorkshire Evening Post*, 14 February 1938.

19 Unpublished letter from Prokofiev to Watson Lyle, dated 16 July 1932, Serge Prokofiev Archive, SPA 9863.

20 Young Pioneers was a mass youth organization established in 1922 for children aged between 10 and 15, designed to instil Communist principles into young people from an early age.

21 See especially Morrison, *The People's Artist*.

22 Ibid., p. 65.

23 'The Composer and the Drama Theatre: Interview with Sergei Prokofiev', in *S. Prokofiev*, ed. Shlifstein, p. 103.

24 Ibid., pp. 103–4.

25 Ibid., p. 104.

26 The Ukrainian-born Krzhizhanovsky was a gifted writer and intellectual who was closely connected with Moscow's literary and theatrical circles. Although he achieved fame for his writing posthumously, he made a living for himself as a playwright and lecturer, writing articles and shorter pieces, while also consulting for Tairov's Chamber theatre. Largely still an overlooked Soviet (now Ukrainian) writer, Krzhizhanovsky worked with Tairov's experimental Kamernyi Theatre in Moscow for almost thirty years. For a recent and intelligent contextual introduction to his work, see especially Alisa Ballard Lin and Caryl Emerson in *That Third Guy: A Comedy from the Stalinist 1930s with Essays on Theater. By Sigizmund Krzhizhanovsky*, ed. and trans. Alisa Ballard Lin (Madison, WI, 2018).

27 Commission for approval of music repertoires, part of the Ministry of Education in the Soviet Union.

28 Nikolai Pavlovich Akimov, an experimental theatre director and scenic designer who was born in what is now Ukraine, is known particularly for his work with the Leningrad Comedy Theatre. Akimov's directorial debut was *Hamlet*, produced for the Vakhtangov Theatre in Moscow. In a recent article, Michelle Assay explores Asimov's intentions in his reworking of the Shakespeare original through an analysis of archival materials. See Michelle Assay, 'Akimov and Shostakovich's *Hamlet*: A Soviet "Shakesperiment"', *Actes des congrès de la Société française Shakespeare*, 33 (2015).

29 Shlifstein, ed., *S. Prokofiev*, p. 110.

30 'A New Soviet Symphony', ibid., p. 104.

31 'The Masses Want Great Music', ibid., p. 106.

32 Prokofiev's personal materials can be found in the composer's fund held at the Russian State Archive of Literature and Art (RGALI), fund 1929. The unpublished notes referred to here are also cited in Morrison, *The People's Artist*, p. 111. Source materials located at RGALI, f. 1929, op. 2, yed. xhr. 111.

33 Dzerzhinsky's opera *Quiet Flows the Don* composed in 1935 was adopted as an examplar of Socialist Realism in music, and earned the composer a Stalin prize.

34 Shlifstein, ed., *S. Prokofiev*, p. 106.
35 Ibid.
36 Ibid., pp. 117–18.
37 Ibid., p. 118.
38 'Semyon Kotko', ibid., pp. 117–20.
39 In this opera Prokofiev also had to make some changes to the nationalities implicated as the Soviet Union's involvement in the Second World War progressed. Initially, the hero Semyon was meant to take arms against the counter-revolutionaries who were designated initially as Austro-German nationalists. After the signing of the Molotov–Ribbentrop Pact in 1939, these revolutionaries had to be changed to Haidamaks, that is, Ukrainian nationalists.
40 Shlifstein, ed., *S. Prokofiev*, p. 216.
41 Having been accused of bourgeois Formalism, Meyerhold was arrested in June 1939 and executed by firing squad in February 1940.

6 Happiness and War

1 Rollo H. Myers, 'Prokofiev and Twentieth-Century Music', *The Listener* (14 October 1936).
2 Prokofiev's output for piano was voluminous and is still a critical component of the repertoire of any contemporary pianist. For more detailed scrutiny of his work, see Boris Berman, *Prokofiev's Piano Sonatas* (New Haven, CT, 2008) and Christina Guillaumier, 'A Genealogy of Prokofiev's Musical Gestures from the *Juvenilia* to the Later Piano Works', in *Rethinking Prokofiev*, ed. Rita McAllister and Christina Guillaumier (New York, 2020), pp. 299–316.
3 Simon Morrison's excellent biography, *Lina and Serge: The Love and Wars of Lina Prokofiev* (Boston, MA, and New York, 2013), explains, evaluates and appreciates the role of Prokofiev's first wife in his life and work. Her incredibly moving, harrowing and powerful story is beautifully elaborated.
4 Morrison, *Lina and Serge*, p. 232.
5 The parallels between the opera and the raging war were undeniable. As time passed, this opera came to represent, at least in the eyes of Soviet cultural bureaucrats, a way of propagandizing for Soviet success in the Great Patriotic War.
6 Olga Lamm cited in Harlow Robinson, *Sergei Prokofiev: A Biography*, 2nd edn (Boston, MA, 2002), p. 392.

7 Katya Ermolaeva presents a critical edition of Prokofiev's opera, in the process illuminating the tortuous revision process Prokofiev underwent over more than a decade while trying to get his beloved work staged. See Katya Ermolaeva, 'Prokofiev's First Version of "War and Peace": Lyrico-Dramatic scenes on the Novel by L. N. Tolstoy Op. 91 (1942)', PhD dissertation, Royal Scottish Academy of Music and Drama (RSAMD), University of St Andrews, 2018, for a fuller account. Nathan Seinen provides an intelligent account of the Sovietization and politization of this opera in *Prokofiev's Soviet Operas* (Cambridge, 2019).

7 The Year 1948 and Its Consequences

1 Alexander Pushkin, *Yevgeny Onegin* [1833], Kindle edn, Pushkin Collection, p. 137.
2 Cited in Harlow Robinson, *Sergei Prokofiev: A Biography*, 2nd edn (Boston, MA, 2002), p. 473.
3 *Seven Mass Songs* for voice and piano, op. 89, premiered in Nalchik in 1941.
4 He had already experimented with folk sound in a previous work, for example, op. 104, *Arrangements of Russian Folk Songs* for voice and piano, and op. 106, *Two Duets*, arrangements of Russian folk songs for tenor and bass with piano, composed in 1944 and 1945 respectively.
5 Simon Morrison, *The People's Artist: Prokofiev's Soviet Years* (New York, 2008), p. 330.
6 Natalia Savkina was able to view the diary and discuss it with the author. The diary remains unpublished and can be viewed only with the permission of the Serge Prokofiev Estate. Personal communication with the author, referred to with permission.
7 'The simple-hearted man with the grey eyes.' Taganka production, Central TV (1991), dir. Juri Rashkin, script by Natalia Savkina.
8 Tabernakulov, Prokofiev's driver, related to Natalia Savkina, said, for example, that the composer did indeed go to the Lubyanka, although it is unclear whether he was summoned there or whether he went on his own initiative and on behalf of Lina. Personal communication with the author, referred to with permission.
9 Prokofiev is buried in the Novodevichy Cemetery in Moscow. Mira is buried with him. She died in 1968.

Select Bibliography

Ахонен, А. Н. (A. N. Akhonen), *Прокофьев в Петербургской консерватории* [Prokofiev at the St Petersburg Conservatory], vol. XIV, St Petersburg Music Archives (St Petersburg, 2016)

Bartig, Kevin, *Composing for the Red Screen: Prokofiev and Soviet Film* (Oxford, 2013)

Berman, Boris, *Prokofiev's Piano Sonatas* (New Haven, CT, 2008)

Blok, Vladimir, ed., *Sergei Prokofiev: Materials, Articles, Interviews* (Moscow, 1978)

Chamberlain, Lesley, *Lenin's Private War: The Voyage of the Philosophy Steamer and the Exile of the Intelligentsia* (New York, 2006)

Clark, Katerina, *Moscow, the Fourth Rome: Stalinism, Cosmopolitanism and the Evolution of Soviet Culture, 1931–1941* (Cambridge, MA, 2011)

Dubinets, Elena, *Russian Composers Abroad: How They Left, Stayed, Returned* (Bloomington, IN, 2021)

Frolova-Walker, Marina, *Russian Music and Nationalism from Glinka to Stalin* (New Haven, CT, 2007)

Guillaumier, Christina, 'Ambiguous Modernism: The Early Orchestral Works of Sergei Prokofiev', *Tempo*, LXV/256 (April 2011)

—, *The Operas of Sergei Prokofiev* (New York and Suffolk, 2020)

Karlinsky, Simon, and Alfred Appel Jr, eds, *The Bitter Air of Exile: Russian Writers in the West, 1922–1972* (Berkeley, CA, 1977)

McAllister, Rita, and Christina Guillaumier, eds, *Rethinking Prokofiev* (New York, 2020)

Maes, Francis, *A History of Russian Music: From Kamarinskaya to Babi Yar*, trans. Arnold Pomerans and Erica Pomerans (Berkeley, CA, 2006)

Mann, Noelle, 'And More on Prokofiev's Three Oranges!', *Three Oranges Journal* (November 1995), http://sprkfv.net

Moisson-Franckhauser, Suzanne, *Serge Prokofiev et les courants esthéthiques de son temps (1891–1953)* (Paris, 1974)

Morrison, Simon, ed., *Sergei Prokofiev and His World* (Princeton, NJ, 2008)

Nabokov, Nicolas, *Bagázh: Memoirs of a Russian Cosmopolitan* (New York, 1975)

Nice, David, *Prokofiev: From Russia to the West, 1891–1935* (New Haven, CT, 2003)

Press, Stephen, *Prokofiev's Ballets for Diaghilev* (London and New York, 2006)

Prokofiev, Oleg, trans. and ed., *Sergei Prokofiev: Soviet Diary 1927 and Other Writings* (London, 1991)

Prokofiev, Sergei, *Prokofiev by Prokofiev: A Composer's Memoir*, ed. David H. Appel, trans. Guy Daniels (New York, 1979)

—, *Dereviannaia kniga* [The Wooden Book] (St Petersburg, 2009)

Prokofiev, Sergey, *Diaries 1907–1914*, vol. I: *Prodigious Youth*, trans. Anthony Phillips (London, 2006)

—, *Diaries 1915–1923*, vol. II: *Behind the Mask*, trans. Anthony Phillips (London, 2008)

—, *Diaries 1924–1933*, vol. III: *Prodigal Son*, trans. Anthony Phillips (London, 2012)

Said, Edward W., *Reflections on Exile and Other Literary and Cultural Essays* [2001] (London, 2012)

Sayers, Lesley-Anne, 'Re-Discovering Diaghilev's "Pas d'Acier"', *Dance Research: The Journal of the Society for Dance Research*, XVIII/2 (2000)

Scheijen, Sjeng, *Diaghilev: A Life*, trans. Jane Hedley-Prôle and S. J. Leinbach (Oxford, 2009)

Shlifstein, S., ed., *Sergei Prokofiev: Autobiography, Articles, Reminiscences* (Moscow, 1959)

Sitsky, Larry, *Music of the Repressed Russian Avant-Garde, 1900–1929* (Westport, CT, 1994)

Taruskin, Richard, *Stravinsky and the Russian Traditions: A Biography of the Works through Mavra*, 2 vols (Berkeley, CA, 1996)

Todorov, Tzvetan, *Introduction à la littérature fantastique* (Paris, 1970)

Zuk, Patrick, *Nikolai Myaskovsky: A Composer and His Times* (New York and Suffolk, 2021)

Select Discography

Below is a selection of recordings of some of Prokofiev's key works. They are listed in chronological order.

String Quartets Nos 1 and 2; Cello Sonata Aurora String Quartet, Naxos (1995)

Toccata, op. 11, Martha Argerich, Deutsche Grammophon (1995)

Music for Children, Olli Mustonen (pianist), Ondine (2005)

The Love for Three Oranges, Rotterdam Philharmonic Orchestra, Chorus of the Dutch National Opera, Opus Arte, DVD (2005)

Ivan the Terrible; Romeo and Juliet, Suites 1 and 2, The Philadelphia Orchestra and Philharmonia Orchestra, Riccardo Muti (conductor), Music Warner Classics, Parlophone Records Limited (2011)

Violin Sonatas Nos 1 and 2; Sonata for two Violins; Violin Concerto No. 2, London Philharmonic Orchestra, Janine Jansen (violin), Vladimir Jurowski (conductor), Decca Classics (2012)

Romeo and Juliet, The Royal Ballet, Orchestra of the Royal Opera House, Opus Arte, DVD (2019)

The Symphonies (includes *Scythian Suite* and others), Bergen Philharmonic Orchestra, Andrew Litton (conductor), BIS (2021)

Piano Sonatas Nos 1–9, Diana Klinton (pianist), Brilliant Classics (2021)

Fiery Angel, Orchestra and Chorus of Rome Opera, Naxos, DVD (2021)

Acknowledgements

I owe so much to so many. This book would not have come to completion without R. Words cannot express my gratitude. Mum, Dad and Stephanie kept the show on the road when I could not.

I would like to thank my wonderful editors at Reaktion Books – Michael Leaman, Emma Devlin and Alex Ciobanu. Thanks to those who have been with me from the start of my Prokofiev journey, quite a few years ago – Rita McAllister, Simon Morrison, Nicolas Moron and Natalia Savkina. The Royal College of Music supported this work in myriad ways and I am eternally grateful. The fantastic Natalia Ermolaev from the Serge Prokofiev Archive was as indefatigable as always.

My thanks also go to Professor Robert Adlington; librarian par excellence Monika Pietras; wonderful colleagues, especially Ivan Hewett, Gabrielle Lester and Diana Salazar; and inspiring students who keep the music alive and bright. Prokofiev's music is safe in your hands.

This new biography of the composer builds on the meticulous work and research of other scholars, especially that of Natalia Savkina, David Nice, Laetitia Le Guay and Simon Morrison.

The Prokofiev family have been supportive from the start. I am grateful to Serge Prokofieff Jr and Gabriel Prokofiev for their tireless patience as I attempted to tell their grandfather's remarkable story.

Photo Acknowledgements

The author and publishers wish to express their thanks to the below sources of illustrative material and/or permission to reproduce it:

Alamy Stock Photo/Lebrecht Music & Arts: p. 54; Bridgeman Images/ Lebrecht Music & Arts: pp. 82, 102; Library of Congress, Washington, DC: pp. 58, 64, 67, 75, 79, 91; photos Serge Prokofiev Archive, Columbia University, New York, reproduced with permission: pp. 31 (SPA 15703), 41 (SPA 15714), 42 (SPA 15702), 50 (SPA 15704), 89 (SPA 15709), 98 (SPA 15663), 99 (SPA 15665), 112 (SPA 15639), 115 (SPA 15627), 117 (SPA 15628), 126 (SPA 15638), 131 (SPA 15667), 132 (SPA 15634), 151 (SPA 15635); TopFoto: pp. 62 (Roger-Viollet), 104 (Heritage-Images); Wikimedia Commons (public domain): pp. 29, 142 (Russian State Archive of Literature and Art, Moscow), 147.